MW01290833

Peacemaking Under Fire
A Vietnam War Memoir

by John Arnold

Copyright © 2011 John Arnold
All rights reserved.

Website: http://www.peacemakingunderfire.com
Contact: info@peacemakingunderfire.com

ISBN: 1463735227
ISBN-13: 978-1463735227

Introduction

In firefighting you aim the hose at the base of the flames. Throughout the early years of the Vietnam War, it seemed like most peacemaking efforts, as genuinely sincere and well-intentioned as they were, were aimed at the metaphorical equivalent of the top or middle of the fire. By September 1968 it was clear, to me at least, that such efforts were insufficient to stop the war. The aim needed to change, and that meant working for peace at the base of the flames, where the war was, in Vietnam itself. So that is what I did.

These may be curious dedications for such a book, but I would like to dedicate it both:

To the memory of Major General George Henry Thomas, the greatest general to fight in the American Civil War, and possibly in all of U.S. history. Thomas was a Virginian who more than any other military leader won the war for the Union, unfortunately under the shadow of Grant and Sherman who used every device at their disposal then and later to denigrate Thomas's achievements, and to claim as much credit for themselves as they possibly could. I am in awe of Thomas's unwavering grace and loyalty in the face of such bitter betrayal, and I hope that someday he gets the credit he deserves.

And to the 5th Marine Regiment of the 1st Marine Division of the United States Marine Corps, a unit I am immensely proud to have served with despite the circumstances under which that service occurred.

Chapter One
In the Beginning

On November 7, 1970, a somber yet celebratory group of people gathered at the Washington Square Methodist Church in New York City to commemorate the 47th anniversary of The War Resisters League, an organization committed to opposing all wars, everywhere, always. As is customary at the annual WRL event, the high point of the evening was the presentation of the League's Annual Peace Award to that individual or group which in the League's opinion had best exemplified its goals and ideals during the previous 12-month period. The winner for 1970 was: RESISTANCE IN THE MILITARY. They promptly mailed me not just one, but two original copies of the award.

Several weeks later, on the other side of the world in Vietnam, my Marine Corps regiment's commanding officer hosted a little "going away" gathering attended by most of the 5th Marines' (5th Marine Regiment, 1st Marine Division) senior officers. At the gathering he awarded me a Regimental Commendation, and sent the room into gales of laughter with an observation that "The war just won't be the same without you!" It had been, as they say, quite a year.

It is now 40 years later, and I am finally feeling inclined to get what happened back then down on paper for whatever use it might ever be to anyone. Perhaps only to future generations of our own family, who I would certainly like to encourage to stand up and actively oppose injustice even in very difficult situations when that is the right and honorable thing to do. But perhaps someday this will reach a wider group, and will help dispel some of the many myths and falsehoods that have grown up about the Vietnam War.

Here are the basic facts and figures of what you are about to read: I arrived in Vietnam on December 5, 1969 at age 19 years, 1 month as a Marine Lance Corporal (E-3) assigned to the 5th Marines (Fifth Marine [Infantry] Regiment) with a generalist "communications" military occupational specialty. The Regiment was headquartered at An Hoa at the time, a failed industrial complex (and reportedly a coal mine, although I never saw any evidence of it) about 50-60 miles out in the bush southwest of Da Nang. We were there for 7-8 months, then we pulled in closer to Da Nang to an old French colonial fort on Hill-37, and finally by that fall we were at Marine Corps Combat Base Baldy along the famous Route 1 south of Da Nang. I left Vietnam on or about November 25, 1970, a full Corporal (E-4) with seven decorations, the aforementioned Regimental Meritorious Mast (that is what the Marine Corps calls commendations), and a share of the War Resisters League Peace Award.

But the story should begin at its beginning, which for me was on November 4, 1950, in Dayton, OH. I was born the third of three children to a very nice couple who, like everyone else in the post-war era, were struggling to catch hold of The American Dream after spending their early years in The Great Depression, and their teenage years in World War Two (my father served in the U.S. Navy on a destroyer in the South Pacific). Over the objections of his parents, who thought it more prudent for him to get into something solid like fixing radios, my dad went to work for an adding machine company called IBM that was coming out with a new line of business machines called "computers". He studied how to fix them, walking to work because we couldn't afford a car.

Shortly after I entered the picture, IBM sent him and us to live for a year or two in Muskegon, Michigan, then for about five years 30 miles or so inland in Fremont, and finally to just north of Grand Rapids, where we stayed through my high school graduation in 1968.

We were a pretty typical family of the era, I think. We went to school, went to church, and watched TV. The men and boys in the family, including both grandfathers, a half-dozen uncles, and some cousins, hunted and fished, more for the fun of being together and outdoors than to seriously try to catch or kill anything. Between my family's many fishing/hunting/canoeing/camping trips and being in the Boy Scouts I became much more comfortable and adept at being out in wilderness areas than I realized at the time, which proved immensely helpful in Vietnam. A lot of my fellow Marines had never been outside a city, and the nights in the bush held just that many additional challenges and terrors for them.

My brother, sister, and I, along with many of our cousins, spent most summers up at a cottage my dad's parents had on the Muskegon River by Big Rapids. We all had chores we needed to do - wash dishes, chop wood, etc., but when our chores were done we were pretty much free to wander the woods and river at will, day or night, in a very laid-back Tom Sawyer-sort of way. At home, I read books endlessly, mostly about history.

In 1964 I attended the Boy Scout National Jamboree in Valley Forge, PA. That was an unbelievably wonderful trip in all kinds of ways; but two incidents from it particularly stand out:

The first occurred on our way there, as our bus wound its way through New York City. It stopped at a stop light, and I glanced out the window and saw, maybe four feet away, an old woman who was ravenously eating garbage directly out of a garbage can next to the curb. I have spent the better part of my life working on the hunger issue because of that moment.

The other was being out on the physical fitness course (where you could earn a badge of some sort) at the Jamboree itself and being approached by none other than Lady Olave Baden-Powell, the widow of the founder of Scouting, who was "afraid that we might be exerting ourselves too much in the hot sun, and should perhaps take a rest in the shade and have tea." It was as though for a moment we were back in Victoria's England, a time that, despite its many shortcomings, also had a charm and graciousness I have always wished had carried forward into the modern era.

We were running pretty short on grace and charm right then. John Kennedy had been assassinated, and the largely uneventful Eisenhower era was giving way rapidly to the Space Race, the Arms Race, the War on Poverty, the Civil Rights Struggle, and a festering little war off in Southeast Asia. Fortunately, in 1964 the voters rejected the militaristic Republican presidential candidate Barry Goldwater in favor of the more reasonable Lyndon Johnson, so at least the war would go away, or so we all hoped.

I was too young to do anything more than watch the news and anguish at my not being able to get involved as the civil rights struggle became THE main thing going on. Some people from the Grand Rapids area went south on the Freedom Ride buses. One of them was the one attacked by a mob and burned while the police stood around laughing. I was absolutely outraged, but quickly learned that there are always new levels of outrage available: At school we had to sit through a government (J. Edgar Hoover and the FBI no less!) propaganda film contrasting how in a democracy like ours the rights of the individual are always respected whereas in communism the government doesn't respect any rights - on the very day that the 6:00 pm news covered the police turning attack dogs loose and fire hoses on people kneeling and praying for the right to vote in Selma, Alabama. It was just unbelievable.

In the 1960's in America, there were people who were oblivious to the changes in the world and in society around them. There were the people who have become the symbol of that decade with flowers in their hair, etc. Finally, there were people who became intensely political: marching, leafleting, petitioning, etc., largely for civil rights and the War on Poverty, and against "the bomb" and later the Vietnam War.

I was very much part of that political group, but not because my family was. One of my childhood memories is of a wall at my dad's parents' house that was almost like a shrine. At the center was a picture of my grandfather in his World War I Navy uniform. Around him were pictures of his five sons and one daughter in their World War II or Korean War service uniforms, and then around them another circle was starting, of my generation in uniform.

At my mom's parents' house there was a picture of her dad in his World War One Army uniform - he had been part of the Polar Bear Division that was diverted from France to Siberia to fight the Bolsheviks. And that was that: You voted Republican. You worked. You paid taxes. You went to church and were involved in the schools and in the community (Masons, Elks, bowling leagues, etc.). And in time of war, you enlisted and served.

Except, I was beginning to have some problems with that way of life. I had bought a big old 1940's shortwave radio at an auction, and on it I was able to pick up English language radio programs from all over the world.[*] I decided to do a project for school on the subject of how truthful governments were. Specifically, I monitored a select set of different countries' English language news programs on the subject of how many U.S. aircraft were getting shot down in Vietnam. What I found stunned me: The U.S. government was systematically falsifying what was reported!

On any given day, the Defense Department would admit to having lost maybe one aircraft. When pressed about communist reports of larger losses - say six planes - the DoD spokesperson would always react indignantly

***

[*] A momentary digression: The auctioneer had said the radio worked, but you never know about that sort of thing. When we got home from the auction, my dad helped me carry the radio up to my bedroom; we plugged it in and with our fingers crossed we turned it on to see if it worked. The tubes in it started glowing, it started making a humming noise, and then without our having touched the tuning knob yet a voice began speaking: It was Franklin D. Roosevelt declaring war on Japan...! Dad went ashen. We both just stared at the radio in incredulity. The President finished his statement, and then a cheery announcer said, "Thank you for listening to today's 'Voices from the Past' program..."

to the "lies the communists tell". Then I'd switch over to Radio Moscow, Radio Havana, or even to the BBC in London, and sure enough there would be "those lies" about six planes. I would carefully record those numbers, stations and dates.

Every single time, within just a few days, the Defense Department would admit that "two additional planes had been lost" on that day. Later they would admit that "an additional plane" had been shot down back then, etc. Within a week to ten days what the Defense Department admitted to always added up to precisely the number those "lying commies" had said had gone down on the day it happened! Does that mean I think the communist governments of that era were always truthful with everyone about everything? Hardly. But that wasn't my problem or concern. My problem and concern was that OUR government was obviously lying to US about a war that was quickly spinning out of control.

The Marines had landed at Chu Lai in 1965, and now hardly a day seemed to pass without the American people hearing that "we'd turned the corner" (meaning we were finally winning), but that more troops were needed over there to put the final nail in the coffin. Day after day, week after week, month after month - same message: We're finally winning, and we need to send more troops. Troops that could only be sent and sustained at the expense of the war that most of we political types wanted to see fought and won, which was the War on Poverty. It and the civil rights struggle were both getting pushed aside more and more so that manpower and money could be diverted to the war in Vietnam.

Meanwhile, there was a coup in Vietnam every

few months, and more and more governments and people around the world had started voicing concerns about what on earth the U.S. thought it was doing there. By about 1965, one also began to hear of "a peace movement" in this country. People much like those who had been involved in the "Ban the Bomb" and the civil rights movements were gathering and speaking out, this time for both peace and justice. In the Midwest, and I suspect across most of America, the common reaction was shock and utter dismay that "such people" should even exist and why don't they just go back to Russia where they belong?

But not everyone felt that way. Some of us heard. Unfortunately, at age 14, in high school, and ten miles out in the suburbs of Bland Rapids, Michigan one could only grind one's teeth and bide one's time.

The only time I recall finding an opportunity to assert my angst at some of the silly/dumb stuff our government was doing was when some organization - I forget exactly who, but likely the American Civil Liberties Union - announced that it was shipping into the United States from "Red" China a bunch of copies of the Quotations from Chairman Mao Tse-Tung, the famous "little red book" read and waved in the air by millions of Chinese during that country's infamous "Cultural Revolution". Either imports from China generally, or that book in particular, were banned by the U.S. Government, so anyone who ordered copies risked going to jail, fines, etc. I promptly ordered six copies, and when my books eventually arrived they were each hand-stamped (on the last page of the index) with a disclaimer from the U.S. Government. But no one ever came to arrest me.

By late 1966, I'd just about had it. Enough was

enough, and something had to give way or I was going to explode with pent-up need to do ANYTHING other than just go to school and pretend everything in the world was just fine. Just then, fate dealt its first interesting card in my direction: I happened to mention to one of my uncles that I was going crazy just going to school, and that I needed to be more involved in the world than that. He suggested that I should apply to work as a Page (errand runner) for the Michigan House of Representatives for its spring session; he was dating a woman who worked as a secretary up there and had just heard from her that they'd recently switched from wanting high school freshmen to wanting high school juniors, which is what I was, and that they'd just opened the application process.

I quickly applied, and much to my surprise I was selected to work what had to be one of the most interesting sessions that anyone ever could have worked there: There was a new governor, a need for the state to finally bite the bullet and pass an income tax, and a House that was split evenly 55-Republicans and 55-Democrats. We worked liked dogs, sometimes from sun-up until nearly sun-up, for six months. It had little to nothing to do with the war or any of those larger issues, but what an amazing learning experience it was! There were hundreds of Bills and Resolutions under consideration, and at least that many Amendments to them; and we Pages were supposed to be familiar enough with all of those proposals and with the individual Legislators so that when one of them (a Legislator) came sprinting in at the last second for a roll call vote they could, with some degree of confidence, holler over to one of us, "Am I for this, or against it?", and we, with some degree of confidence, were supposed to know and holler back the answer, and they would vote whichever way we told them to.

Bottom line: Our government has lots of flaws, but most people involved in it are sincerely interested in doing "the right thing", and good guys sometimes do come out on top. It really is an amazingly wonderful system, which is something I never could convince some of my more jaded political friends of. And that was the difference between a lot of them and me. I'd worked with government firsthand and came away believing in the process, while many of them never did.

About four months into that adventure, fate tossed out another card: It seems the good folks who made Wrangler-brand blue jeans were growing increasingly concerned about how anti-American a lot of our allies overseas were seemingly becoming, and so they came up with a plan that was a wonderful marriage of marketing and marketing! The concept was to dress up about 100 squeaky clean American teenagers in Wrangler clothes and send us to bicycle around Europe showing those silly Europeans what America and Americans really were like. I applied, with the Speaker and the Clerk of the Michigan House of Representatives, and then-Congressman Gerald Ford's brother Tom, who was a State Representative, as my character references. They accepted me, and as soon as the legislative session ended it was time to pack my bags and head overseas!

They gathered us in New York, flew us to London, got us our bikes, split us into groups of about 8, and sent us on our way. My group sailed across the English Channel to Denmark, rode across it to wonderful Copenhagen (where two of us split off and took a boat to Sweden for a day), then south into Holland and then Germany.

We boarded a river boat and sailed down the Rhine River 100 miles or so before getting back on the road again through more of Germany, some of France, and on into Switzerland. From Geneva we rode a train to Paris, and from there a rode a train to Brussels. In all, we visited eight countries in about eight weeks, staying in youth hostels, eating bread, wine, and cheese, except when pastry shops had something more delectable to offer out on the road, wandering without supervision (our group's leader quickly developed an intense dislike for all of us and promptly abandoned us whenever we reached a town where we were to stay for more than a day) through the capitals of Europe during the summer of 1967... What more can I say?

...EXCEPT that it was probably the most radicalizing experience any of us possibly could have had. It may have been the "Summer of Love" for some, but for us it was endless late-night discussions in hostels, cafes and pubs with people from all over the world, both the developed and developing parts of it, at the very apex of the revolution that was the 1960's. What we learned was that the United States had positioned itself on the wrong side of the liberation struggles of the 20th Century in general, and in Vietnam in particular. Indeed, the U.S. Government was systematically lying to the American people about Vietnam and the Vietnam War, and we became collectively outraged by that.*

---

* Once they saw that their experiment had created a planeload of anti-war activists, the people at Wrangler pulled the plug on what they had hoped to make an annual event. But here it is 40+ years later, and faithful as a hound dog I still buy and wear Wrangler jeans, always! It was a truly incredible trip, and I shall always be grateful to them for making it possible.

By the time I got home that fall (the fall of 1967), the 1968 Presidential race was just getting under way, and I quickly started supporting Eugene McCarthy, a maverick U.S. Senator from Minnesota who was going to challenge the sitting President from his own party, largely on the issue of the war. In the late fall/early winter (weeks before the New Hampshire primary) I patched together a completely ad hoc organization that won the Michigan High School Student Mock Democratic Convention for McCarthy by acclamation on the second or third ballot. It was all make-believe, but those were times for making dreams into dreams-come-true, and the fact that McCarthy had so much support did lead to Johnson's eventual decision to withdraw from the race.

In the meantime a carry-over from my Lansing days was beginning to play itself out in the form of my launching an underground newspaper - West Michigan's first so far as we know - to give voice in our high school to issues the "official" student newspaper couldn't or wouldn't touch. While in Lansing working at the Capitol, I'd run into the alternative/underground newspaper from Michigan State University, and through it I'd discovered many others like it around the country.*

For the times, my paper wasn't terribly political or radical - it focused more on school issues than anything else - but it was an outlet that let me survive until graduation, and actually taught me a whole lot of skills that would later prove very helpful.

---

*   If you ever see any movies about people making a revolution, one of the scenes almost certain to show up is one where the revolutionaries give voice to their radical new ideas via the steady "whump, whump, whump" of whatever sort of printing press they'd been lucky enough to get their hands on.

My favorite memory of the paper was that after we'd missed about a month in getting an issue out, a teacher asked me if I had any idea what had happened to it? I assured him that of course I had no firsthand knowledge of the matter (because who exactly was putting it out was obviously secret), but that rumors had it that the people who were putting it out were buying all the paper and everything out of their own pockets, and had apparently run short on funding... He paused a second, asked me to wait for him, and disappeared into the Teacher's Lounge, returning a moment later with a handful of money that he pressed into my hands, asking me if I'd try to get it to the correct parties...? Interesting times!

One other high school event of note: I didn't particularly care about sports, but it was still nice my senior year when our school's previously terrible football team finally started winning some games for a change. In fact they were tied for the league championship, and were to play the team they were tied with at our school's Homecoming. Then it started snowing, and the night before the day of the big game we got 12-14 inches of snow. By the time we got to school, the word was out that the game would be canceled because of the snow. Because it was a home game, this would mean that our team would forfeit, and that the other team would be named the league champions by default.

In our first class of the day I kept talking about how unfair that was beyond the limits of the teacher's patience. He told me to keep still because the game couldn't be played, and that was that. I persisted in my protests. So he (this is the same teacher who gave me the money for the underground paper) asked me what I thought should happen? I said that the game should be played. He pointed out that the game couldn't be played with snow on the field. I said that we should get the snow off the field. He asked how that miracle ought to occur? And I said that snow shovels are the traditional way...

The minute the words were out of my mouth, I realized that I had just made a terrible mistake. He got a gleam in his eye and indicated I should come with him. He took me to the janitors' room and asked them to give me a snow shovel so I could go shovel off the football field. And then he sent me out there, indicating I should not return until the job was done...

You know, when you get right down to it, football fields are really big. It certainly looked big that day. I trudged out to the corner of what I supposed was one of the end zones, leaned on the shovel a moment pondering my fate, and then noticed out of the corner of my eye that hundreds of people (other students) were watching me from their classrooms. So I started shoveling. A few minutes later a guy came out from one of the boys' gym classes, and asked, "What are you doing?" I said, "Shoveling off the football field." He asked, "All by yourself?" I paused in my shoveling and theatrically looked around, and affirmed, "So far." He asked, "Can we help?" I told them that they could if it was okay with the gym teacher.

Within minutes those 30-40 people joined me, followed by the girls' gym class, at which point all the doors of the school were leaking people and herds of them were running up to me and asking if it was okay if they ran home quick to get their snow shovels, etc. I would appear to seriously ponder the matter, and then would agree to their doing so (which, of course, I had no authority to do!) "if they would come right back". Ultimately the entire student body turned to, and by about the third hour we had a cleaned-off football field. The game was played, and our team won.[*]

Another incident I suppose I should mention (confess to?) was the day my friend Ken King and I skipped school. It was spring in our senior year and he and I, both of us honors students and him, I believe, even the President of the Student Council (and I can finally make known: my primary co-conspirator in putting out the underground paper), were in the High School Library working on an Independent Study project we were doing together when one of the girls' gym classes walked right past the window. We asked where they were going, and they said they were going bowling and that we should come too.

It was too tempting, so for the first and only time in our entire school careers we snatched up our books, bolted out the "do not open except in emergencies" door, and got on the bus with them. As it pulled out of the parking lot we glanced over saw the High School Assistant Principal, Gordon Johnson, was watching us from window of his office with a very puzzled look on his face.

We got to the bowling place, which wasn't very far

---

[*]   I actually ended up doing very little of the shoveling myself, by the way. Once a couple hundred people were out there digging and sweeping I decided that some music would be a nice touch, so I walked purposefully into the front office and told the secretary to announce on the PA system that members of the school's pep band were to immediately report to the band room with their instruments and jackets, and then I quickly exited the office before anyone could ask me any questions, such as what the heck I was doing? I got my trombone and led the pep band out and we sat in the bleachers playing the school song, and various other pep band sorts of tunes while the field was cleared.

from the school, and went in, but the gym teacher who we'd had in a class of some sort and who liked us still wouldn't let us bowl, so we decided we'd better just go back to school. We got back and went to our next class. Before the teacher got there an announcement came over the PA system: "John Arnold and Ken King, please report to the office."

Ken got up and then noticed that I had not. He said "We have to go." "No." I said, "I'm not going." "What!?!", he shot back. "If they call you have to go." "No", I repeated. "If they call it only means they have called. It doesn't mean you have to go." He gave me a long, critical stare, and declared, "You are certifiably crazy, and you are going to get into a world of trouble." And off he went, leaving me clinging to my desk chanting "Hell no, I won't go!" I'm not sure what they said to him, but he ended up beating the chalk dust out of erasers for at least a week afterwards. They never called for me again, and Ken never quite forgave me for it. We played tennis all the time, and he cursed me every time we did for not getting my just desserts for that skipping incident.

Graduation day finally came, and while many of my classmates wept and hugged, I couldn't stop grinning while packing my bags. Two days later I was en route to Wyoming and a summer geology program the University of Michigan ran out there: It was about 8 weeks of hiking up mountains, into caves, onto volcano cones, up onto glaciers, down to hot springs, etc. - it was not only great fun, but also fulfilled my entire math/science requirement for a pre-law bachelor of arts degree!

I flew back to Ann Arbor to start the fall term, and came through O'Hare Airport in Chicago on the first day of the infamous Democratic National Convention of 1968. Revolution was definitely in the air, along with a lot of smoke, sirens, shouting, and tear gas!

In Ann Arbor I immediately linked up with the SDS (Students for a Democratic Society) chapter, and spent a totally crazy couple of weeks shuttling between the two crises it was simultaneously involved in: treating and comforting the wounded returning by the busload from Chicago, and dealing with 1,001 things related to a huge welfare rights strike that had several thousand people demonstrating/rioting in Ann Arbor itself. I did actually attend a class or two in the midst of that, but it quickly became clear to me that my student days were effectively over. I just had no stomach for sitting around in a lecture hall when there was so much going on in the world that was infinitely more important.

Unfortunately that put me in much the same difficult position that SDS and other similar groups were left in by Hubert Humphrey's victory/Eugene McCarthy's defeat in Chicago. Having failed to stop the war by holding teach-ins, by holding prayer vigils, by circulating and signing petitions, by marching in marches, singing songs, blocking doorways and roadways, burning draft cards, and going to jail, trying to elect a pro-peace candidate had been the radical left's last evident strategy option. An incredible funk settled over the organization and the entire anti-war movement.

While I wasn't necessarily in a funk myself, I did need to make some decisions: I was in school largely on scholarships which more or less anticipated that one would actually attend classes, and in a few months I would be turning 18 and would need to, theoretically at least, register for the draft. There was no way I was going to do that,[*] but that meant probably going to prison or to Canada, but I wasn't keen on either of those options. I wanted to stop the war, not just become one of its various sorts of victims, and so I was very much up in the air about what I should do.

Only years later did I discover there are other people like me, who more or less give themselves up to being used as tools in the hands of whatever the heck power it is that more or less tries to manage the fate of people and nations. Most people refer to that power as "God". I don't, because the voice that has spoken to me hasn't made a big deal about what its name is and because the word has gotten loaded down with too much right-wing baggage, but it is that same force.

The peer group I eventually discovered was the Religious Society of Friends (Quakers), and by the late 1970's I'd formally become one, but in the fall of 1968 I was on my own and badly in need of some guidance from upstairs.

Now the deal with opening oneself up to "leadings", which is both very cool and also very much the reason that most people can't do it, is the fact that you stand a pretty good chance of getting one, but with almost a 100% certainty that it will be something that you hadn't even considered as a possibility. Never was that more the case than with me during those crazy few weeks at U. of M.

The SDS chapter essentially imploded on itself in an anguished effort to figure out what to do next. It was very, very intense, with many, many hours of heated

[*]   In my opinion military conscription is a human rights violation of the first magnitude, and I was committed to having nothing to do with it whether there was a war or not.

debate. The most newsworthy thing to come out of those sessions was a group of people who decided that the only way to end the war was, in their words, "to bring the war home" by engaging in acts of war here in America against certain individuals and institutions. The idea was that their targets needed to feel some of the sort of pain that was being inflicted on the people of Southeast Asia in order to understand that what the United States was doing in Vietnam was wrong and needed to stop. This group came to be known as "the Weathermen" or later as "the Weather Underground".

I felt no tug in that direction whatsoever. It left me stone cold, and still without the direction I needed. Fortunately good old fate has its ways of filling such vacuums, and in my case it conspired to have me attend a campus film series showing of the movie *Doctor Zhivago*.

For anyone unfamiliar with the film, *Doctor Zhivago* is about some people whose lives get all wrapped (and messed!) up in the Russian Revolution. Partway through the movie, the storyline drifts over to the impact that World War I had on those times and people. The scenes themselves are of the Russian forces marching proudly off to war with flags flying and bands playing and then taking a terrible beating at the front, with a voice-over about how the Reds saw the war as an essentially inconsequential struggle of the bourgeoisie - no matter who "won" it, the winner would still be standing on the backs of the people. But, the narrator went on to explain, the Reds all enlisted in the armed forces anyway "BECAUSE IT WAS IN THE ARMED FORCES THAT THEY COULD DO THE ORGANIZING THAT WOULD BRING ON THE REVOLUTION".

I literally fell out of my chair. That was it! THAT was what we needed to do! We needed to enlist and organize there, in the very heart of the beast!

I went screaming back over to the Student Activities Building where the SDS offices were and talked with anyone who would listen, and was pretty much universally met with looks and reactions of disbelief, which after a while cooled even my jets a little. I mean seriously, to enlist in the armed forces and try to organize a revolution there? That does seem a bit extreme – and not only could you get yourself killed, but you could very easily get yourself killed!

Having slept on it, I got up the next morning resolved to actually attend a class or two. But on my way across the big central plaza there on campus it hit me like a ton of bricks: "You can't stop a war if you are not where the war is." I stopped, pondered that for a moment, walked over and dumped my books in the trash, and went up to the Admissions Office and dropped out.

Making the phone call to my folks was a little harder. "Hi, mom! Oh, no, everything here is fine... How about you? Well actually there has been a little change of plans. Instead of staying in school and becoming a lawyer I'm flying home in the morning to enlist in the Marines..."

They actually took it pretty well.

Chapter Two
Into the Marines

I flew to L.A. (my folks had moved there during the summer) and my mom dutifully took me down to the Marine Corps Recruiting Center where I had an interesting exchange with the top guy there. After I'd filled out all their forms with stuff about being an honors student and having been a page in the legislature and touring Europe and attending U. of M. entirely on scholarships, etc. he looked at them and then at me, and asked, "So what do you want to do?" And I said, "Enlist for three years." He looked at me, hard, and said, "No you don't." And I said, "I don't?" "No," he said, "you don't."

He was the first of many very highly principled people I encountered in the Corps. Although his own career was dependent on his ability to attract and sign up the best people he could get his hands on for the longest time periods he could talk them into, he really thought I could and should do better with my life than devoting three years of it to what they had to offer, and he said so. We went back and forth about it for quite a while, and ultimately I signed papers for both two and three years. When I reported in to the big Armed Forces Induction Center in L.A. a week or so later they, apparently being a little less highly principled, tore up the two year papers, and so I went in for three.

Allow me to digress here to explain my actions a bit more thoroughly. I picked the Marine Corps instead of one of the other branches of the military for two main reasons: First, they were the only ones who could/would guarantee that I would go to Vietnam, which is where I needed to go in order to do whatever the heck it was that I was meant to do. And second, because to the extent that I had any notion of what that calling might be, it seemed like the Marine Corps was a better vantage point than anywhere else. If I spoke out against the war, the fact that a Marine was doing so would carry greater weight than say, some Army guy stationed in Germany, or some Navy guy aboard some ship. Plus, if a revolution was to be launched, the Marine Corps seemed like who I would prefer to have leading it instead of opposing it!

Seriously though, my overriding concern was that the American people simply weren't getting the straight scoop on the war. The government was feeding them lies, and I hoped that if those lies could be countered by folks the American people might be inclined to believe, like active duty Marines in or just back from Vietnam, they would stop the war. It kind of goes back to my firm belief in the basic goodness of the American people and our form of government. I believed that if the American people got the truth about the war they would do the right thing about it, so I needed to be where I could help them get that truth.

An important secondary consideration, which relates to the Marines being the only branch that would get me out into the thick of things in the war, was the remote possibility that once I got over there I might find that the anti-war movement was wrong, and that the war was, in fact, just and proper. Then, as above, being a Marine would position me both to fulfill my duties as a citizen and earn the right to have my picture up with my granddad's and dad's, and to communicate THAT message from an equally advantageous vantage point.

Some people have asked me in later years if I ever seriously entertained the notion that the war might be "right" and that I might reverse my role and become a champion for it, and I can affirm that I did. I grew up in the 1950's when the idea of questioning the government (questioning Ike?!?) was totally off the radar screen. Like most Americans of the time, my ingrained bias was to believe our government; it was the distrusting and disbelieving part that was so wrenching and difficult.

Why three years instead of two? Essentially I was concerned about simply not having enough time to do whatever needed to be done. Two years seemed awfully short when you figured that two months of it would get used up at boot camp, another month at infantry school, two more on leaves, at least a couple more in whatever occupational specialty school they might send me to, and probably another one in traveling. It was no good trying to get off cheap. If I was going to do this thing I needed to do it right. I hoped that meant three, because I could have gone in for four, but that seemed beyond what even I should/could set myself up to try to endure (and my quiet little guiding voice agreed).

Multiple people asked me how I could agree to become a "murderer"? I would counter that I had no intention of becoming a murderer. They would protest that if I were ordered to shoot I would "have" to do it. And I would laugh. There was/is simply no power in heaven or on earth that could make me pull a trigger I didn't feel I should pull. Period. Regardless of the consequences. I never gave up, nor ever anticipated giving up, the Nuremberg Trials-affirmed responsibility to make one's own ethical judgments, even in the heat of battle.

Lastly, was I concerned that this little escapade might have some of the same sorts of side-effects that they list on a lot of medicines: Dizziness, disorientation, trouble breathing, heart irregularities, liver damage, and other conditions including death? Yes. Generally I was more aware of the possibility than concerned about it – though there were certainly particular moments of heightened concern along the way! About the same time I was doing all of this, one of the popular rock bands released an album with a title of, if I remember correctly, "No One Gets Out Alive", and that seemed to me to nicely describe the situation all living things are in. If we live, our dying sometime is a given. That being the case, it is far better to live for something, to have one's life have meaning, than to slink away and hide from what needs to be done in hopes of scrabbling a few extra days or years of life from that. If you are going to talk the talk, you need to walk the walk. That is all I was doing.

On induction day there were about 400 of us. We got weighed and measured and poked and prodded, with all of the drama and trauma one might expect of that time and that occasion. There were people who had been fasting, or gorging themselves on bananas, or getting "Fuck You" tattooed on the part of their right hand that would be facing out if they ever had to salute anyone, or taking other steps in the hope of being disqualified. Lots of others (including me) just moved through the process more or less resigned to our fates. The most excitement happened when they announced to the people being drafted that day which of them were going to the Army (cheers!) or to the Marine Corps (groans of disbelief). I saw many a man cry that day.

Ultimately we raised our right hands and swore - although few of us repeated what the guy up front was telling us to repeat after him ["I state your name do solemnly swear..."]. Myself, I was continuing my conversation with my inner guide about how I hoped to all goodness that s/he knew what they were doing because this situation was rapidly moving beyond a point of no return...

After the swearing in, we were loaded onto buses for the 3-hour trip* down to the Marine Corps Recruit Depot in San Diego. There was a lot of brave talk on that bus. Talk of how somebody had heard that Drill Instructors were real jerks who would try to push you around if you let them, and how the speaker wasn't going to let them push him around, etc. But when we passed through the arched entranceway, all of that brave talk drifted away like the morning mist, to be replaced by the silence of the living dead. People along the sidewalk pointed at the bus and laughed.

It was dark. The bus pulled up by an L-shaped building. In the opening of the L, there were yellow footprints painted on the cement, about four feet apart, in straight rows, all facing the same direction. We stared at those as though transfixed, for what was probably only five or ten minutes but seemed like hours. Then a door of that building opened and the meanest-looking S.O.B. ever to walk the face of the earth stepped out and marched across those footprints to the door of our bus and climbed up in it and faced us.

---

* It may have more or less than that; I think I was going into shock, and time no longer had meaning for me.

He stood rigidly at attention but eyed us as a predator might eye its next victim, and then his mouth opened and out upon us spewed the bile of a thousand years, that we were the sorriest-looking #%$&}#@{}%$#@# bottom of the barrel scrapings it had ever been his misfortune to have to deal with and if we didn't haul our sorry asses off that bus and plant our feet precisely on those painted foot prints within the next five seconds he was personally going to disembowel and stomp to death the entire lot of us... MOVE! MOVE! MOVE! And scurry like little mice we certainly did. We ran for our lives!

Without needing to be told to, or even how to, we all stood rigidly at attention, no one daring to breathe. In a few minutes one or two other people - official Marine Corps people - came and talked at us. I remember they told us that our rights and dignity as human beings and as American citizens would always be respected, and that if we ever felt that we weren't being treated fairly we should feel free to complain about that up the chain of command. And then they left.

As they left, the face of our original greeter transformed from stoic non-commitment into something truly hideous, and it snarled, "You are MINE now...!" And indeed we were. He was to be one of our three drill instructors. He drove us into the L-shaped building, where our hair was cut off and clothing thrown at us, and then we were told to kneel down along the walls of a big room facing the wall, and to breathe. We were told that if we did anything else without permission we would die. Then he very slowly directed us to remove each article of our clothing, item by item, one at a time, and replace it with the Marine Corps-issue goods piled in front of us.

A few minutes into that exercise we all heard someone get up and walk across the room to where the drill instructor was and say, "Hey, I didn't get any socks!" It was, I can only think, like that moment between when you realize that what is falling toward you is an atom bomb, and when it goes off. Time stopped. And then there was a sound much like a watermelon might make upon hitting the pavement from, say, three stories up. There was that sound, the sound of a body hitting the ground, and then the kicking of that body, and its screaming, and the drill instructor screaming at it that it had been told to kneel and breathe, and to do nothing else without permission!

Many people were spattered with blood from that incident, and I noted with some interest that none of the people who had affirmed their plan to stand up to a drill instructor chose that moment to do so. I know that I certainly did not, but I had not bragged that I would. Heck, if he'd told us to kneel and NOT breathe, I'd have done my level best to comply!

A short digression on the subject of Marine Corps Boot Camp: The theory behind it, I am told, is to toughen people up and to sort them out by subjecting them to worse pressures of all kinds than they are likely to experience in combat so that "those who can't hack it" can be sorted out from those who apparently can. It's a nice theory, but in reality one simply does not know how one will react in combat until one is in combat, and the sorting process described above seems to me to be a failed experiment. In my own experience, almost half the people in any given unit under fire malfunction in one or more ways. Most often, people simply freeze up. The second most common quirk is fixing on some activity, such as putting a clip in a rifle, and doing it over and over again. Others stand up when they should get down, or talk when they should shut up, or cry or pray or holler out stupid questions ("What should we do?!?" ...What do you think we should do when people are shooting at us?). It's true that I never saw anyone throw down their rifle and run away, so maybe the sorting works in that sense, but what a pain in the butt to have half the people around you nonfunctional when you are wishing fervently that you had twice as many people as you do!

In pursuit of its "sorting", the Marine Corps takes great pride in how horrible its boot camp experience is for its recruits. I can affirm to you without qualification that no story you ever hear about something that is alleged to have happened at a Marine Corps Boot Camp is too awful to be true, and that it has not changed. I add the second point because one of the things that current and former Marines who are jerks, as well as totally unprincipled recruiters, like to tell new and prospective enlistees before they report to boot camp is that while it was "bad" "in the old days" "it is different now". It is not different now. It was and is a process remarkably similar to the creation of the orc armies in the Lord of the Rings movies.

The days in boot camp began well before sunrise with a drill instructor turning on the lights and screaming at everyone to immediately jump out of bed and stand at attention. Then they'd dismiss us to go wash, shave, etc., periodically turning out the lights, turning off the water, and/or turning off the hot water all or part of the way through people's getting showered and shaved. The fact that there was no light or water was no excuse later in the morning when we got inspected; you'd better be clean and clean-shaven, or God help you! Likewise, if the D.I.'s found that someone forgot to flush the toilet, they would form us in a big single-file line leading from that toilet, and we would have to hand from person to person whatever had been left in the toilet until someone identified it as being theirs.

Southern California notwithstanding, it was cold in San Diego at 4:30 am or whatever ungodly time it was we finally went running out to stand at attention in front of our barracks. We would stand there shivering for 15-20-30 minutes, and then a drill instructor would come out and ask if we were cold? If we answered that we were, we would then be put through a grueling routine of exercises, including doing push-ups on our knuckles on the gravel, to help us warm up. If we answered that we weren't cold, he would say that was good, and go back in their office for another 20 minutes or so to have another cup of coffee, leaving us standing out there freezing to death.

Meals were a time of chow hall staff piling whatever they were serving on your plate and then of you frantically gobbling it down with a drill instructor looming over you shouting, "Eat! Eat! Eat!" Leaving anything on your plate or asking for seconds were obviously out of the question. People have asked me, "How was the food in boot camp?", and my honest answer is that I have no idea. Meals weren't about food; they were about getting whatever was on your plate off your plate as quickly as you possibly could.

Many recruits were not initially in good physical shape, and woe onto them. Not only would they be beaten for not keeping up (three-mile run in combat boots), or not doing enough push-ups, but if you showed any fear or hesitation on the obstacle course it was as likely as not the drill instructor on hand would knock you off whatever thing you were on with a long pole, and if that sent you to the hospital, as it did several people, too bad!

We had classroom type classes mixed in with all of that, on how to clean a rifle, how to salute, how to shine shoes, why you shouldn't get venereal diseases, some basic first aid, etc., and eventually we had a practical application test on all of that. There were ten testing stations, and as you went to each one you'd be confronted with something you needed to know or do: take apart and reassemble a rifle, apply appropriate first aid to a simulated wound, etc. I was the only person in our platoon who got a perfect score, which was the only time I truly messed up in boot camp. Fortunately coming to the attention of the drill instructors that way did me no harm. As crazy as it sounds, it really could have! In boot camp you never wanted to be noticed for any reason, good or bad.

Part of what got me through boot camp was hanging out with another recruit by the name of Francisco Wellington, III, who was the son of a Bethesda, MD psychiatrist, and had been drafted into the Marine Corps. He was in total denial that such a ridiculously inappropriate thing should have occurred, and regularly had me in stitches laughing at his indignation and disbelief. Whenever they paired people up to do something - practicing saluting one another, practicing lunging at one another with bayonets, etc. - he and I would always link up. While all around us people lunging with their bayonets would be screaming "Die!" and "Kill!", etc., Francisco and I would be shouting "Peace!", "Love!" – of course not so loudly that the drill instructors could hear. I never saw or heard from him again after infantry school; I hope he did his two years and got out okay. He really helped me keep my sanity.

The only day or time we had relatively free was Sunday morning, but even that got somewhat messed up by the fact that you had to profess to being a Christian, and had to go to church services, or the drill instructors would want to know why not, and that was a discussion you did not want to be part of. After church we could sit outside on our footlockers and write letters, read, etc. for a couple of hours without getting yelled at or beaten.[*]

There wasn't much overt racism in boot camp, but I was taken aback by how often drill instructors used feminine terms to berate us: "Are you ladies cold?" "You cunts had better..." "Now girls..." I will also never understand why they went to such lengths to convince people that "their old lady was screwing long-haired Jody" while they were in boot camp. Over and over and over again we would hear about how Jody was enjoying the money people sent home, how Jody was enjoying driving their car, how Jody was living the Life of Riley at their expense. I don't really know what the point of that was, but we heard it all the time.

---

[*] This led to my experiencing one of the most incredible sights of my life: The Marine Corps Recruit Depot is right next to the San Diego Airport; only a chain-link fence separates the two. One Sunday morning when we were sitting out there someone suddenly yelled, "He's not going to make it!" All eyes turned toward the airport where a big passenger plane, a jet with its engines back at the tail, was obviously in the midst of overshooting the runway. As we watched, the pilot realized what was happening and did something I have never seen another plane ever do, and didn't know they even could do: He jerked the plane's nose up in the air, fire came out of those engines, and it literally took off like a rocket, shooting up over the mountains that were not far from the end of the runway. The ground shook and the roar was incredible, and I bet those engines went into the repair shop afterwards, but he got the job done, and earned a big cheer and a round of applause from us.

- 31 -

The other person we heard about a lot was 'John "Chickenshit" Wayne'. Never 'John Wayne', but always 'John "Chickenshit" Wayne', as the ultimate fake hero. While many movie stars, musicians, etc. entered or worked with the armed forces during World War II, apparently Mr. Wayne made movies instead, and the Marine Corps has never forgiven him for it.

Another surprise was how overtly boot camp promoted smoking: In the Marine Corps, a rest break was called a "smoke break," and the people who did smoke were permitted to spend smoke breaks standing around chatting and smoking. Those of us who didn't smoke were generally ordered to 'police up' the area around where the smokers were smoking, which meant scouring the ground for other people's cigarette butts to pick up and put in the trash.

After a week or so of that, every person in our platoon started buying, carrying, and lighting up cigarettes every time we got a smoke break. Not everyone actually smoked the lit cigarette they were holding, but we were all holding one, and many people did develop an addiction to that nasty habit as an alternative to being made to clean up after people who already were addicted to it.

The one thing I will give the Marine Corps Boot Camp experience credit for is that it does instill a pride that will never leave you. Ever. No matter who you are or whatever else you might ever do. You were a Marine. You made it. You survived one of the toughest endurance tests there is for mortal human beings, and in surviving it you are privileged to join the lists of those who "stormed the halls of Montezuma", who shut down the Barbary pirates, who stopped the German advance on Paris in World War

One, who took back island after island in the Pacific, and who chewed up a dozen Red Chinese divisions in breaking out of the Choson Resevoir in Korea. As a member of that small elite group of fighters, you will never surrender and you will never run. You might well die, but you will never surrender and you will never run.

How deep does it get under your skin? If you've read this far, you know of my biases and predispositions coming into all of this, and that I came out of the war hating it more than when I went in. But while I was in Vietnam, I took a radio message from five Marines who were with a Vietnamese company out on patrol, who reported that they'd been ambushed by what they estimated was at least a battalion of the NVA (North Vietnamese Army), that the ARVNs (South Vietnamese Army troops) they were with had run away, that the five of them had taken advantage of the element of surprise to launch an attack of their own and had wiped out two machine gun nests, and that they now wanted air and artillery saturation of their entire sector, which, of course, meant that they were absolutely certain to die. I could not feel anything but pride that when the shit had hit the fan they had performed as Marines. THAT is how much it gets under your skin.

Anyway, boot camp was a blur of very unpleasant experiences, although I came through it less bruised and battered than most. I quickly learned that if you did exactly what they told you to do, you tended to come out okay. Amazingly, a lot of people apparently never grasped that. The drill instructor would no sooner say "No talking!" than some idiot would feel compelled to tell someone next to him about a letter he'd just gotten from his girlfriend. Or they would tell us to polish our shoes, turn their backs, and 50% of the people would get out something to read or their letter-writing gear! An amazing number of my peers just couldn't seem to figure out that, if you did what you were told, you didn't get beat on; and if you didn't do what you were told, you did get beat on. It seemed to me to be a pretty straightforward concept.

There were still little hidden land mines you could run afoul of anyway: For example, when drill instructors talk to an individual recruit, they like to shout or snarl directly into the recruit's face. This tends to be unsettling, and in such a situation it is easy to forget that a Private (that is the rank we all were) in boot camp is not ever supposed to refer to him or herself as "I". If you do, the drill instructor's conclusion is usually that you must think that you are a "private-eye", and they will then make you crawl for miles on the hot tarmac with your nose pressed to the ground "looking for clues".*

You could also call attention to yourself by asking to go to the bathroom, asking to go on sick call, or, God forbid, getting anything that indicated it was your birthday. If the latter happened, the drill instructors would eat the cake and then make you eat the box it came in!** For Thanksgiving we had a truly wonderful, very traditional feast, and then they took us out and exercised us until every single person had thrown it all back up again and had buried it with their bare hands. Happy Thanksgiving!

There were several other incidents of note I will mention before we move on:

---

*   What you are supposed to do is refer to yourself in the third person as "the Private", as in, "Sir, the Private requests permission to ask a question, sir!"
**   I had my 18th birthday in boot camp, but at my pleading, no one sent me anything.

HOW NOT TO PASS AN INSPECTION

One day our drilling (marching practice) went particularly badly, to the point of driving our drill instructors into a frenzy - which was never a good thing. I forget everything they did to punish us, but I know that they had us put our hats on backwards, untuck our shirts, carry our rifles upside down, link arms, and skip back to our barracks area while singing something like "Polly Wolly Doodle All a Day". Once back there, they had us bury our rifles in the dirt out front, throw all of our clothes out of our footlockers onto the floor, dump all our bedding onto the floor, and then dump buckets of dirt on all of that. At that point, word came down that a V.I.P., the base commander or some similar person, was going to be holding a surprise inspection of our barracks in five minutes!

There was nothing we could do. We were doomed. And so we stood rigidly at attention, with our hats on backwards and our shirts untucked, up to our knees in dirt, clothing and bedding as he slowly walked through. He didn't say anything. None of the folksy/fatherly banter about, "Where are you from, son?" like you see in the movies. This was that "moment between when you see the bomb and when it goes off" deal all over again. And when he left, it did.

The drill instructors went insane. I don't recall precisely all that happened, but part of it was our being instructed to pull the mattress covers off our mattresses and to put them on over our heads (so that we looked like ghosts), not so that we would look funny, but rather so that we couldn't see the freight train before it hit us, adding the uncertainty of "what, when and where" to the certainty that it would, indeed, be hitting you. Then they ordered us to start running in circles, tripping over beds, footlockers, each other, etc., and started in on us themselves, hitting and kicking and cursing and screaming and knocking things over.

At least seven people were hospitalized. Within the week, three more attempted suicide, one successfully, and some unknown number literally lost their minds and/or attempted to escape.* As for myself, I don't know whether it was one or two people who, when hit by a drill instructor, staggered or fell back into and onto me, but however it happened I ended up under a pile of what seemed to be dead people, and in the finest traditions of those who survive mass murders, I elected to stay quietly there until the killing stopped. It proved to have been a wise decision, and I got away with it.

THE MESSMAN FROM HELL

About halfway through boot camp, Marines go spend a couple of weeks at the rifle range. In our case, that meant going from San Diego up to Camp Pendleton. The first week you are there they assign you to a work detail of some sort, and I ended up working in the chow hall,

---

* Fairly early on in boot camp our drill instructors did a presentation for us on "How to succeed in committing suicide," on the rationale that "If you are chickenshit enough to not be able to hack it (boot camp), you probably are so worthless the world would be better off without you, so if you want to commit suicide here is how to do it successfully." They really did walk us through the mechanics of taking aspirin to thin the blood, of using the sharpest cutting edge available, and cutting down the length of the arm instead of across it, etc. The recruit who succeeded reportedly followed those instructions almost exactly.

washing dishes. The chow hall was huge and fed thousands of people, but had enough dishes and silverware for only a fraction of that, so during meal times we frantically tried to keep ahead of demand lest we suffer the attentions of the person in charge, who we quickly came to know as "The Messman From Hell". He was, if anything, even more of an unreasonable jerk than our drill instructors were, and we were his for about 17 hours a day.

Despite the fact that there would not be any dishes to wash until the first chow lines opened up several hours later, everyone assigned to work in the chow hall had to report for duty at some ungodly hour, which I believe was 4:00 am, so that those who actually prepare food could do so. Our day would end when the last dish was washed, generally between 8:00 and 9:00 pm.

In the meantime there we were, a crew of about a dozen miserable recruits inhabiting one of the two sculleries (dish washing rooms) the chow hall had. The first thing The Messman From Hell did upon receiving us, after he'd gone through all the standard insults about what pieces of rancid whale crap we all were, etc., was to tell us that our every moment at the chow hall was to be spent productively, either in washing dishes or in cleaning the scullery. Under no circumstances were we ever to just sit or lay about. He wanted the scullery (which was a smelly, dirty pit) to just sparkle. When he left, we posted a guard and slumped to the floor.

This went on for a day or two, and then the smell and look of the place started to get to me. The wall opposite where I was sitting was particularly getting on my nerves. It was an ugly, dirty testament to what happens if a wall never gets cleaned in a place where dirt, food, and grease constantly get tossed around. I sat there looking at that ugly, dirty wall until I just couldn't stand it any more. I considered moving so I could look at a different wall, but they were all just as bad. I finally decided that it was the wall or me, so I got up and got a pail and ran it full of soapy hot water and found a sponge and went over to the wall and started washing it.

The others in the group stared in disbelief. Finally one of them asked, "What are you doing?" And I said, "I am washing the wall." And he said, "Why?" And I said, "Because I can't stand looking at it any more the way it is." And he (on behalf of the group) hurrumphed, "Don't expect anyone else to help you!" To which I shot back, "So who asked anyone to? Go back to sleep and let me do what I need to do."

That was that for a few minutes, except that under all those sad, sorry, ugly, stinking layers of neglect I was uncovering a rather pleasant white wall, first only in a small spot, but then bigger and bigger. At which point another sponge plopped into my bucket and one of the other guys asked, "Mind if I help you? Beats sitting around..."

"It does," I affirmed, and as we worked we started chatting - the first real conversation that had taken place in that miserable tomb. And then another sponge showed up, and a couple other people got up and said, "Hell, the dish washing machine looks and smells like crap too. We might as well clean it." Just a few minutes into that, someone remarked that it was full of brass pipes that would really polish up pretty if somebody worked on it, which someone promptly jumped up to do.

Before long, the entire crew was up and working, and the more we worked the better the place looked, and people really started getting into it, genuinely having fun, laughing and talking, and improvising ways to get up high enough to be able to wash the windows and the ceiling, even crawling under the dishwashing machine to polish the brass fittings under it! Then, without warning, the door burst open and into the room sprang The Messman From Hell, come to catch us napping!

He looked in complete incredulity at the startlingly clean walls, and at the people polishing the ceiling, and at the sparkling floor and at the sparkling dish washing machine with people draped all over, in and under it with various sorts of cleaning materials in their hands, and his mouth just kind of hung open. Finally he managed to gasp, "What are you doing?" "Cleaning?" I ventured.

He stared with incredulity at what truly was an astonishingly clean room, and then refocused enough to ask, "Why?" "Because you told us to?" I suggested. "No," he said, "Nobody does what I tell them to." "Okay," I said, "this area was really dirty and needed a good cleaning, so we decided to do it." He nodded, his mouth alternately opening and closing without words coming out. Finally, he stammered a "Carry on!" and left.

Within what seemed like only two or three minutes he was back, marching the entire chow hall crew, including the cooks and other permanent staff, to stand at attention and see what we had done while he berated them up one side and down the other for what miserable pieces of various sorts of excrement they were to be so badly shown up by a group of raw recruits who on their own initiative had done such a wonderful job because it was the right thing to do, and that by god we were his fair haired boys and for the rest of the week we were to be treated like princes of the court and he would personally kill anyone who ever dared show us less than the utmost respect!

The rest of our week in the chow hall, was, I am pleased to report, a very pleasant respite from the rest of boot camp.

AT THE RIFLE RANGE

After we finished our week at the chow hall, they spent several days showing us how to properly hold, aim and (without ammo) shoot the M-14 rifle from standing, sitting and prone positions.* Then we started going to the rifle range with live ammo to practice shooting from 100, 300 and 500 meters.

Being at the rifle range was incredibly stressful for all concerned. The drill instructors were painfully aware that 70+ people who hated their guts now had weapons and live ammo, so they were really edgy. As you might expect, edgy drill instructors are even more prone to beating people than normal drill instructors are. We recruits were all pretty stressed because of the above, plus the fact that not shooting well almost guaranteed visits by the drill instructors' fists.

They got us up at the usual ungodly early hour - it was late November/early December, so the days were really short then - and by the time we'd marched a mile or two to the rifle range the sun would just be coming up. One of those mornings, as we trudged from the 500 meter firing line to the 100 meter firing line where we'd start shooting for the day, some bird started chirping out just the jolliest song you've ever heard. It must have had

---

*   An M-14, of course, is not even remotely like an M-16, which is what we were subsequently issued in Vietnam.

worms aplenty and eggs on the nest to be so cheery. We, the walking dead, endured two or three minutes of that bright happy cheeriness, and then someone, speaking for the entire lot of us, screamed at the top of his lungs, "FUCK YOU, BIRD!", nearly rendering us incapable of shooting we were all laughing so hard.

Once we did get down to some serious shooting we were each assigned a shooting coach (generally an infantryman back from Vietnam waiting to get out) to help us properly adjust our rifle sights, etc. That worked well enough until the day we were firing for scoring purposes and my coach showed up blotto drunk.

Now, being drunk on the rifle range is a world class offense, but I couldn't very well say anything to anyone. Instead, I just tried to make the best of it, doing what he told me to do when it made any sense at all and faking it when it didn't. At 100 meters you can usually hit the target no matter what, but at 300 meters there is no margin for error, so I started missing the target quite a bit.

After probably the third or fourth miss I heard him begin a curse, and when I regained consciousness I was on my back surrounded by drill instructors and other rifle range officials who were waving smelling salts under my nose and examining the growing lump on my head Apparently my "helpful" coach had smacked his spyglass down on my head after that last miss, knocking me out cold. That called some attention to him, which promptly ended his coaching career. So now their big worry was whether I would recover well enough to continue shooting. I did, and they were very nice to me about it, even though I didn't do all that well.

WHO ARE YOU
AND HOW DID I MISS BEATING YOU?

There are 80,640 minutes in an 8-week boot camp. Some of those minutes pass more quickly than others, but they all do pass one way or another, and so like all things, boot camp does eventually end. As it wound down to the last day or two, our drill instructors began to show a human side they had not ever shown before. They broke down and talked with us (with the group, not with individuals) now and again, almost as if they and we were of the same species or on the same side in the war.

But danger was never far off. One of those last days as we stood in line out in front of the chow hall waiting our turn to go in, our platoon's head drill instructor suddenly grabbed me by the throat and demanded, as he choked the life out of me, to know why I was trying to sneak into the chow hall with his platoon?

As the world began getting dim I managed to gasp out, "Sir, the Private belongs to this platoon, sir." This caused his hand to loosen slightly and him to ask others around me, "Is that so? Is he one of ours?" They all quickly affirmed that it was true. He let go, looked at me very quizzically, and told me to "Carry on."

The night before we graduated, the drill instructors got our platoon together for a chat. At one point one of them expressed a hope that we would remember them fondly, which sent a ripple of laughter through the room. "What?" he demanded, "Why wouldn't you remember us as being your friends?"

"Because you beat on us?" some brave soul suggested. "Naw... well maybe a few of you sometimes, but only a little now and then," the DI retorted. When that was also greeted with laughter, he asked for a show of hands of how many people had gotten beaten. Almost every hand in the room went up.

The drill instructors looked at each other in seeming incredulity, as though they really were surprised they had hit that many people - they who had sent over 20 of us to the hospital, the brig, the mental health ward, or the morgue. One of them somewhat more weakly asked, "Who didn't we beat?"

It took an act of faith to raise one's hand in response to that question, because for the next 16 or so hours we were all still fair game to make up for lost opportunity. But five of us did raise our hands, prompting the DI's to ask, "How did we miss you?" And in every case the story was the same: We did what we were told to do. We never called attention to ourselves. And we were very lucky.

The drill instructors took all of that in, and then advised everyone else to stick close to someone like us in combat, because we were going to be the ones to come back alive.

WRAPPING UP AND MOVING ON

Thinking back on it as an educational experience, boot camp was more or less a wash. Some things we did there later proved useful, particularly learning the Marine Corps' history with all the pride that comes of that. On the other hand, I never did find knowing how to salute, polish shoes (particularly the soles of shoes!), march, or accurately shoot an M-14 rifle to be particularly helpful when I was up to my neck in a rice paddy pinned down under fire as I tried to get my stupid M-16 to un-jam. In all, probably 90% of boot camp was spent on traditions that were nice but of no earthly use whatsoever to people about to go off to engage in jungle warfare.

Chapter Three
Infantry Training & Communications School

As we were told 1,001 times, "Every Marine is first and foremost an infantryman." So, before they try to teach you anything else, they want make sure you have a pretty good grounding in battlefield operations. That way everyone knows what to do if they ever have to throw the Divisional Band into the breach, which I understand that the First Marine Division had actually done during the Tet Offensive earlier that year. So off we went to Camp Pendleton again, but this time as Marines and not as Marine recruits.

Our four weeks in infantry school, also known as ITR (Infantry Training Regiment), proved to be only slightly better than boot camp, although a nighttime beating of one of our particularly obnoxious handlers by person or persons unknown (I was not involved) quickly established that they were not drill instructors and that we were no longer recruits, and that we were done with putting up with that sort of b.s. forever.

This is not to say that ITR was without its ups and downs. For example, one of the things we had to do was run an obstacle course that contained a solid wall about 9 feet high. The idea was to run up to it, leap high enough to get one arm over the top, and then haul yourself, your rifle, etc. up over it unassisted by anyone else. Unfortunately, I have a lead butt. It doesn't leave the ground no matter how highly motivated it might be to do so. I told them that, but do they let me just skip that part, or let anyone help me? Of course not! I spent half a day bouncing myself off a wall over and over for no particular purpose.

Two particularly noteworthy events happened at ITR. The first was something that had really begun in boot camp, but which in ITR rose to a crescendo: An expression of utter contempt for the Vietnamese people in general and for the women there in particular. Over and over and over again we were admonished by various trainers in various ways that "the gooks" weren't really people, and that their silly language and even sillier traditions were nothing we'd ever need to worry about, and that the only good use for the women there was "you know what...!"

Our trainers were all Vietnam veterans and they tried to out-do one another with stories of the torture, rape, mutilation, theft, arson and mayhem they had gotten to engage in. The more bloody and outrageous the story, the more the crowd ate it up, hardly able to wait to participate in such festivities themselves. "This is not how I would prepare troops to 'win the hearts and minds of the people,'" was my silent observation.

The drill instructors and ITR trainers also heaped endless contempt on participants in the anti-war movement, but I had expected that. What I had not expected was to be taught the rule of thumb that, "If it is Vietnamese and dead, it was a VC." This was essentially an open invitation for we who were to go to war on behalf of the Vietnamese people to simultaneously wage our own personal wars against those very same people without fear of being called to account for any crime we might ever elect to commit against them. I felt utterly betrayed by a system that was supposed to be teaching its participants how to win a war where how we interacted with the civilian population was likely to prove of critical importance.

Almost a flip reverse in some ways was what happened when they made us give up a weekend's shore liberty in order to be able to attend (attendance was mandatory) a "patriotic" choir concert that some fundamentalist civilian church in the area wanted to put on "to show their support for our troops and the wonderful job they are doing."

We were young men away from home; many of us for the first time, and with money to spend and the easy booze and easier women of Tijuana only a short bus ride away. Giving that up to hear a bunch of church people sing at us was not exactly on our to-do list!*

But we had our orders from the Base Commander: If churches wanted to entertain troops to show support for the war, then troops would be entertained, and as the lowest troops on the proverbial totem pole, we were to be the lucky recipients of that show of heartwarming support.

---

* I never did go to Tijuana. It was a town utterly dragged to the depths by the proximity of thousands of young Marines and Sailors (the Navy also has a boot camp in San Diego). Booze, drugs, and sex in every way, shape, and form it can possibly come in were the attractions, in addition to plenty of opportunities for bar fights for those drawn to such festivities, which an amazingly large number of people were. Instead, four of us drove well past Tijuana to the sleepy little coastal village of Ensanada in hopes of finding peace and relaxation for a few days. Even there some ladies of the night made a determined effort to help us part with whatever money we might have brought with us, rubbing up against us and suggesting that we buy them drinks as a prelude to us all "having a good time." One of my buddies, without batting an eye, said, "I'm hungry! Let's eat first!" snatched up a cockroach that was wandering across the tabletop, and ate it. Apparently the ladies of the night of Ensanada have some standards, because at that point they fled from us never to return.

Then they told us that the frigging hymn sing couldn't come to us; we had to go to it, and that it was clear over on the other side of the base (which is huge), and that there were no vehicles to transport us. So off we went, hundreds of pissed off Marines herded like cattle for about 15 miles on a hot summer afternoon in order to be lined up as an audience for 30-40 totally clueless middle-aged church people singing about how Jesus loves us and our war. I never felt so sorry for a group of performers in my life. The kindest audience response I heard the entire evening was "Fuck you!"

Our handlers were obviously not pleased and tried to be hard on us on the way back, yelling at us and telling us that we were going to be punished. This lasted until someone yelled, for the first of many times I was hear it, "WHAT ARE YOU GOING TO DO, CUT OFF MY HAIR AND SEND ME TO VIETNAM?" which set people to rolling on the ground with laughter. I mean seriously, we who are about to die have precious little else to fear.

The next thing, as silly as it was, was almost better: Someone quacked. Like a duck: "QUACK!" By then it was pitch black so the handlers couldn't see who did it, but they were furious and stopped the whole column and demanded to know who has dared exhibit this behavior!?! At which point the entire column instantly turned into one giant flock of ducks with each and every throat vying to out-quack its neighbor. I'll bet they could hear us five miles out. QUACK! QUACK! QUACK! QUACK! QUACK!

I know my more orthodox socialist brethren will find such a show of undisciplined behavior (Is quacking on the approved slogan list?) upsetting, but if the entire group had launched into a rousing rendition of "The Internationale" it could not have sounded sweeter to me than those thousand voices quacking in joyful and very open rebellion. There was hope!

All though boot camp and ITR I had studiously avoided going to sick bay, in boot camp because it wasn't worth the trouble, and in ITR because I never really got sick. But when a buddy of mine and I heard what our platoon was going to have to endure on the last training day, we decided we owed it to ourselves to take a break. We both feigned illness and went off to happily sit in a huge air-conditioned waiting room while the rest of our platoon went out and endured a 15-mile hike with full packs and tear gas and all manner of other unpleasantness.

It was a lark for us, but the longer we sat there the worse we both got to feeling. When the doctors finally got to us, they whisked him off immediately to the hospital, and declared that I had both walking pneumonia and the Hong Kong Flu and should be hospitalized as well. What I wanted most in the world was to get away from the Marine Corps for some much-needed rest, so I begged off that my folks lived by the Long Beach Naval Hospital (which was only untrue by ten miles or so) and that if I got to feeling worse I would go get admitted there. They let me go, and the next day we graduated and all dispersed to the wind for our first real break since the beginning of boot camp. I do not remember that leave at all, I was so sick.

After a week or two of leave everyone had to report to whatever occupational training school they'd been assigned to. I was surprised and dismayed to discover that though I'd scored terribly on both the mechanical and electronics aptitude tests they'd given us, some rocket scientist had decided that I should spend an entire year at the Marine Corps Recruit Depot in San Diego learning how to be a communications equipment repairman.

This assignment posed several problems for me: First, I can barely tie my shoes, so there was no way I was ever going to be a competent repairman of anything. Second, I had joined the Marine Corps in the belief that I needed to be where the war was in order to stop it, so rotting for a year in San Diego would do me no good at all. Third, of all the horrible places in the world a Marine can be stationed, being at one of the Recruit Depots comes close to topping the list because of how spit and polish it is all the time. And fourth, fixing communications equipment is something that likely would be done "with the beer and the gear in the rear," which is Marine Corps for "in a protected rear area and not where any sort of action is going on," which, as with being in San Diego, would do me no good in stopping the war.

I asked them to consider switching me to something else, anything else! But no, a technician I would be. My Plan B was to flunk out as expeditiously as possible, just fail, with the assumption that they would then put me somewhere else. With that in mind, I dutifully reported in as ordered, only to find out that not enough people had arrived to justify starting a class and so we would all have to spend a few days just twiddling our thumbs. So we did, occasionally getting base liberty, which I took advantage of to go play tennis (my favorite sport) against myself in one of the many handball courts the base had for some reason.

The interesting thing about those little jaunts across base was what happened when one chanced across some totally terrorized recruit who'd been sent off to sick bay or someplace and had now gotten lost trying to find their way back to their platoon. They lived in utter terror, and no amount of soothing, comforting reassurance could get them to stop screaming "Sir!" before and after every sentence, and just relax and let you help them get to wherever they needed to get to. They'd scream answers to your questions, stand rigidly at attention, and march after you, but that was about as far as the social interaction ever went. I felt so sorry for them, and was so glad that the ones I found had at least been found by someone who would genuinely help them and not just mess with their heads. God only knows, they didn't need any more of that than they already were enduring!

Eventually enough people showed up to start our training. I believe we had one class before they told us that there had been a change of plans. The Marine Corps had decided it no longer needed quite so many electronics equipment techs, and instead needed more communicators, more personnel trained to actually operate teletype, radio, radio telegraph and telephone systems. We dutifully picked up our gear and walked across the base to that school. This was a much better assignment; not only would it train me to do work often done in forward combat areas, but it would also train me to do work handling information, which sounded like a good way to learn what was going on in the war, and best of all, it was only six weeks long!

Comm School was pretty uneventful, being distinguished only by two things: First, in order to train us how to print clearly, they issued us kindergarten alphabet penmanship books, complete with drawings of apples for the letter "A", cute little bunnies for the letter "B", and so on, with little arrows showing how you start the letter

"A" with your pencil down on the bottom line and then you draw up at an angle to the right to the next line and then sharply down at a similar angle to the right back to the bottom line and then you lift the pencil off the paper and draw a line straight across the cone you have made at about its middle point. We were told that, for as long as we were in the Marine Corps with a communications occupational specialty, we were to do ALL of our writing, both professional and personal, according to the strict dictates of that book.

The idea was to keep us in practice at making all letters and numbers so clearly that if, for example, we were killed while writing down a vitally-important radio message, anyone else could pick up our note pad and be able to clearly and accurately read everything we had written. So we boot camp hardened, battle-ready Marines spent endless hours writing our ABCs according to the apples and bunnies and carrots of our alphabet books. We also practiced typing, in case we were assigned to teletype duty, and received a smattering of training with Morse code, semaphore (signaling with flags), wiring, radios and telephones.

The other thing of note from Comm School was an incident that occurred during one of the weekly parades. The parades were basically giant awards ceremonies; the base's personnel would stand at attention while the Base Commander pinned medals on people, and then all of us would march in review past the medal recipients while bands played, etc. It was actually kind of grand in a Pomp and Circumstance sort of way, but, as was so often the case, they managed to ruin what could have been a nice thing.

The problem was that the General would want the ceremony to be held alongside the 8:00 am flag raising, so he'd tell the Colonels to have everyone ready to go by 7:30, just to be safe. The Colonels, none of whom wanted to be the one whose men arrived late, would tell the Majors to have everyone there by 7:00. Of course no Major wanted to be late either, so the Captains would be told to get everyone there by 6:30. The Captains would tell the Lieutenants to have everyone there by 6:00, and so on down the chain of command. The result was that by about 4:30 am, 10,000 people would be lined up out on the tarmac with nothing in the world to do but get yelled at and harassed for three hours while waiting for the silly ceremony to start. It was NOT a good breeding ground for espirit de corps, patriotism and good humor!

When we finally got close to the actual beginning of the ceremony, the officers would start scurrying around getting everyone ready, which meant ordering us up to "Attention!" from the "Parade Rest" position in which we had spent the last few hours. Among the commands barked out along the way from the one pose to the other is "Platoon! Stand By!", generally followed by a pause, and then another command actually changing the way you are standing or holding your rifle or whatever.

On one particularly obnoxious parade day they had gotten as far as "Platoon! Stand By!" when, from somewhere out in the middle of the thousands of miserable Marines, a voice boomed out in an absolutely perfect W.C. Fields imitation: "Ah yes, here we are standing by, an entire group of bystanders...!"

There was an instant's dead silence as everyone stood frozen in shock, and then the laughter started, and all the tension of all the indignities we had suffered in boot camp and at ITR and at having to stand around for hours waiting for silly ceremonies was released in the form of 10,000 people laughing themselves silly to the point of falling down and just screaming with laughter without the ability to stop even if anyone had wanted to.

The people in charge did their level best to bring the situation under control, but ultimately, with the protocol of the mandatory 8:00 am flag raising requiring everyone there to be quiet and standing at attention, which they could not achieve without first ordering us to "Stand By!" again, which certainly wasn't going to work, they gave up and dismissed hundreds of us at a time just to be rid of us.

My class graduated from Comm School in March of 1969. We all got our first promotion, to Private First Class, and orders to our first permanent duty stations, which in my case turned out to be with a ground-to-air missile unit at the Marine Corps Air Station in Cherry Point, North Carolina.

Chapter Four
Cherry Point & *Head On!* / *Wish!*

Whoever coined the phrase, "Getting there is half the fun!" clearly never dealt with military bases and the provisions made for troops getting there. In this instance, the Marine Corps flew me from San Diego to New Bern, North Carolina on a regular commercial jet, which on the face of it doesn't sound too bad. Unfortunately, because it was still "the winter," we military personnel had to wear our winter uniforms, despite the fact that it was incredibly hot and deadly humid on the plane. We then flew through a thunderstorm, which made most of us air sick, and arrived in New Bern in the pouring rain in the middle of the night, where our luggage was unceremoniously dumped onto the dirt next to the two-stall-garage-size terminal building they had at the time.

Dying of the heat, soaking wet, and tired, I dragged myself into the terminal to ask about a bus to the base. No bus. Cabs? No cabs. How, pray tell, then do people get from here to there? "Oh, usually out in the parking lot there are some local 'good ole boys' drinking beer and listening to music in their cars and you can go make a deal with one of them usually…"

Right! I mean have you not seen the movie Deliverance? There was no way in hell I wanted to put my life in the hands of some beered-up 'good ole boy' on the back roads in this godforsaken place in the middle of the night - but that is precisely what we had to do. There was no other option, and not arriving at your new base when ordered to is a serious offense.

So out we went to the parking lot, in the rain, in the middle of the night, tapping on windows and negotiating with big beefy beery good old boys about how much a ride to the base might cost. And those were big, ugly-ass cars. Big honking Buicks with Confederate flags on their bumpers. I did it, and lived to tell the tale, but I have always wondered, what if I had been black? Or female?

May the fleas of 1,000 camels infest the hairy parts of any military base commander anywhere who ever subjects his or her charges to that sort of totally unnecessary stress and humiliation! Buy a damn bus and give your people a ride!

The Marine Corps Air Station Cherry Point, North Carolina was the home base of the 1st Marine Air Wing, and one of three Marine Corps bases clustered in the coastal lowlands of that state. Besides Cherry Point, home to jets and missiles, there was the Marine Corps Air Station New River, which was helicopters, and Camp Lejeune, a huge infantry base.

I was assigned to a Cherry Point unit whose offices were a couple of miles away from the base headquarters and the enlisted housing area. Naturally, they made no provision whatsoever - not even sidewalks - for we lowly enlisted folk to get back and forth from out there. So we walked on the gravel shoulder of the road, and while we were walking, we had to salute any passing car with a gold sticker signifying that it was an officer's car, no matter who was actually in it.

This was a base full of pilots, all of whom are officers, and it turned out that my unit's offices were halfway between the officers' housing area and the main base area. Sometimes I would see so many officer's cars on my way to or from work that my arm would actually start to go numb from saluting! I began to have fantasies of building a metal frame to hold my arm up in a permanent salute. What really ticked me off was that maybe only half of those cars actually had officers in them. The other half were full of their snot-nosed kids, their Great Aunt Agnes, or God knows who, and we had to salute every frigging one of them. But I digress.

I lived in a large barracks that held about 50 bunk beds with wall lockers next to them and footlockers under them. There was no privacy or any options regarding when lights went on or off or much of anything else, just a hundred Marines all sharing the same big space. It was not actually too bad, although there was one incident of note while I was there:

During the summer it got very hot and muggy, little things started getting on people's nerves, and everyone got very edgy. Then a big race riot broke out at Camp Lejeune, which focused some of that edginess in a racial direction. One night I was sitting on my bunk (top bunk) writing a letter when someone complained to the Corporal of the Guard that some black guys were playing their radio too loud. He told them to turn it down. They protested that they had to have it loud in order to drown out that "hillbilly" music some other people always seemed to get away with playing too loud. In the midst of the general hubbub that followed, which involved some additional people from both sides who decided to involve themselves in the conversation, someone said something stupid and the Corporal responded with an incredulous "Oh boy!"

Unfortunately the only part of that which carried through the entire barracks was the "boy!" A full-scale riot broke out, with dozens of people punching and shoving, cursing and wrestling all over the place. A friend on the upper bunk next to mine, who happened to be black, had also been peacefully writing letters. We looked at one another and I asked, "Would you like to fight?"

"No, but thank you so much for asking," he laughed.

So we sat it out, including the part when dozens of MPs stormed the place and clubbed, slugged and wrestled everyone (all the people who were fighting) into submission and hauled bunches of them away. The barracks looked like a bomb had hit it. The whole thing was a pretty interesting spectacle!

MARINE AIR CONTROL GROUP 28

The unit I was assigned to, Marine Air Control Group 28 (MACG-28) was a ground-to-air missile defense unit, or so I gather. I was with the unit for nearly a year and I never really had contact with anyone associated with it except the communications platoon, so I really don't know for a fact that there even was anyone else in the unit or what the heck they might have been doing!

Under normal circumstances I would have been assigned to work watches in the Group communications center, taking in and sending out teletype messages about nothing much of consequence. But my security clearance hadn't come through yet, so instead I got assigned to staff (to be the peon doing the typing and making the coffee) in the Group Communications Platoon offices, working directly with and under I believe it was a Major and two Master Sergeants. The Major and one of the Master Sergeants were okay; the other Master Sergeant was an S.O.B. who quickly demonstrated just how wrong things could go if allowed to:

He was some kind of Hispanic - I forget what - and he hated anyone and everyone Hispanic who wasn't what he was. So when a Hispanic Sergeant who wasn't whatever the Master Sergeant was got assigned to us, he was doomed from the start. A reasonable person would have cut him some slack: He was just back from Vietnam where he'd gotten a Purple Heart and at least one "heroism" medal (maybe a Bronze Star?); he had a good record, and was at Cherry Point to finish up the last 4 or 5 months of his enlistment and get out. No problem, right? Wrong. The Master Sergeant made life hell for the new guy, singling him out for special uniform inspections, calling the communications center to see if he'd shown up for work on time, etc. Every time he found anything he could possibly write the new guy up for, he did. For having a button unbuttoned, showing up for work one minute late. Etc.

In the midst of that, the Sergeant filed an appeal to the Platoon Commander that he was being harassed. The C.O. reviewed the matter, concluded that what was going on was wrong, and ordered the Master Sergeant to back off. This totally infuriated the Master Sergeant, who redoubled his efforts to "get" the guy. Eventually the Master Sergeant got him reduced in rank to Corporal and had still more charges pending. When the C.O. left for a couple of weeks for some reason, the Master Sergeant pulled out all the stops - only to be abruptly slapped on the nose when the

C.O. walked back in unexpectedly to pick up something he'd forgotten. The beleaguered Corporal happened to see him, and again appealed for relief, and our furious C.O. dressed down the Master Sergeant in front of the whole office.

But then the C.O. left, and the Master Sergeant became like a crazed animal; it had become a matter of life and death for him that he destroy this other person, and within a few days the Corporal gave up and took off, going AWOL. He reportedly got as far as New York before he ran out of money, tried to rob a store or something, got caught, got sentenced to prison there, and had a Marine Corps trial for desertion waiting for him whenever he got out. And throughout that whole miserable ordeal there wasn't anything that any of us could do but watch in helpless misery.

However, a short time later, the S.O.B. Master Sergeant finally got his: One day he announced that we needed to repaint the interior and exterior of the Communications Platoon headquarters building. He ordered a bunch of paint, including a lot more than we needed, and some colors we were surprised to see, but what was even more surprising for us was to see the Master Sergeant loading that extra paint into the trunk of his car.

We knew he lived off-base, and quickly realized that that was probably where he was headed with the paint. A call was put in to the front gate, his car was searched, and he too found his career summarily cut short. That didn't do anything to help the guy in New York, but at least it kept us from having to kill the Master Sergeant, which was the other option under active consideration in the platoon at the time.

I'd arrived in Cherry Point in early April of 1969, and had begun chafing to get on with stopping the war, but few opportunities were forthcoming. Periodically they would post opportunities for people of particular ranks and occupational specialties to volunteer to be reassigned to Vietnam, and I put in for all of those I qualified for, but to no avail.

What I got instead was a month's duty in the mess hall. As in boot camp, serving in the mess hall was a miserable but survivable experience. The only thing of note that happened during those interminable 30 days was my noticing a guy also assigned there for the month who wore very non-military round wire-rim glasses. I don't recall ever talking with him, but it struck me that he was someone who also had not fully bought into the Marine Corps' culture.

I had only been back at my regular job for a few days when I walked into the office and found everyone clustered around something on one of the desks expressing all kinds of outrage and dismay about it. I peeked in to see what the offending thing was and was taken aback to see that it appeared to be an anti-war, anti-military, underground newspaper that claimed to be produced by active duty Marines! (Only I heard the angels singing!)

When everyone else had muttered away, the newspaper disappeared into my pocket. Upon closer perusal, it turned out to indeed be exactly what I had supposed it to be: It was an underground newspaper put out by Marines from Camp Lejeune who were looking to partner with other Marines at Cherry Point and New River.

They had a PO Box you could write to and, ignoring the possibility of it being a trap, I immediately sent them a note. It seemed like forever, but a week or so later I got a call from someone who invited me to meet with them at such and such a place on base the next evening.

The caller turned out to be the guy with glasses from the mess hall; apparently he and a couple other people besides me at Cherry Point had also replied to the newspaper, and the newspaper folk had contacted him and asked him to more or less coordinate our next steps. Everyone seemed pretty cool, so we set out for the town of Swansboro where the Camp Lejeune people had rented an apartment to serve as their home base for putting out the paper.

The apartment was the upstairs of a gas station on the edge of town. We all trundled up there, and were surprised to find just a couple of people lounging around in a rather druggy haze. It turned out that the founding staff (four tank crewmen back from Vietnam) had been decimated after publishing the most recent edition of the paper: Naval Intelligence had finally figured out who they were and had seen to it that they were given early discharges, reportedly going so far as to have the County Sheriff drop one of them at the county line with a warning never to come back. In other words, what we had walked into was an exceptionally messy apartment and a nearly complete staff vacuum.

Within a minute or two of our finding all of that out, Steve (the guy with glasses) sat down at a typewriter where a half-finished article was languishing, and started typing. I looked around at the piles of documents, un-opened letters, back copies of the newspaper and other newspapers, asked no one in particular if I could straighten the place up, and promptly began doing so. With that, Steve and I became the new co-editors of Head-On! / Wish!, the Marine Corps' first anti-war newspaper.

Insofar as I have been able to reconstruct events, the first Vietnam-era underground newspaper by or for GIs was *RITA Notes*[*] published at or for the U.S. Army base at Heidelberg, Germany in 1966. *RITA Notes* was followed by three more papers in 1967: *The Bond*, the newspaper of the American Servicemen's Union, an effort to unionize the armed forces, and two papers out of Chicago, *Veterans Stars and Stripes for Peace* and *Vietnam GI*.

You can tell how feelings were running by the fact that in 1968 21 more papers joined those first 4, in 1969 the total grew to 92, in 1970 there were 129 GI papers, and in 1971 the movement peaked at no fewer than 153 GI anti-war underground newspapers in business.

As previously mentioned, the first paper that was clearly Army was *RITA Notes* in Heidelberg in 1966. The Marine Corps came next with *Head On!*[**] starting at Camp Lejeune in December, 1968. The first Navy paper I am aware of is *OM*, which one totally crazy seaman assigned to the Pentagon started putting out in April, 1969. About a month after that, the Air Force joined the pack with *Harass the Brass* out of Chanute Air Force Base in Rantoul, Illinois.

Among the papers that sprung up across the country and around the world were *Aboveground* from the underground Army facilities at Ft. Carson, *A Four Year Bummer* which joined or replaced *Harass the Brass* at Chanute Air Force Base, *Blows Against the Empire* out of

---

[*]   RITA standing for [Resistance or Resisters] In The Army.
[**]   I have always assumed that "Head On!" is a phrase with particular meaning to tank personnel.

Kirkland AFB, *Dull Brass* at Ft. Sheridan, the *Fort Polk Puke* out of Ft. Polk, *Free Duluth* on the USS Duluth, the *Hunley Hemorrhoid* on the USS Hunley, *Left Face* at Ft. McClellan, the *MacDill Freek Press* at MacDill AFB, *Marine Blues* for San Francisco-area Marines, *The 99th Bummer* from the 99th Bomber Group at Westover AFB, *Offul Times* from Offutt AFB, *The Oppressed* at Walter Reed Medical Center, *Pay Back* at the Marine Corps Air Station El Toro, *Pig Boat Blues* on the USS Chicago, *Potemkin* on the USS Forestal, *POW* at Ft. Ord, *Rough Draft* at Ft. Eustis, the *Scaggie Aggie Review* on the USS Agerholm, *The Star-Spangled Bummer* out of Wright-Patterson AFB, *Strike Back* at Ft. Bragg, *Travisty* at Ft. Travis, *Truth Instead* at the Marine Corps Base Treasure Island, *We Are Everywhere* on the USS Coral Sea, *Your Military Left* at Ft. Houston, and dozens more, all speaking out for GI rights, for stopping the war, and a myriad of other causes that were collectively The Revolution.

As I went through the piles of paperwork at the apartment I found all the earlier editions of the paper, lots of completely or partially written articles that had never been used, and much correspondence between the founding staff and a host of other people. There were letters from the other GI newspapers that existed at the time, and from people on other bases who wanted to know how to get started producing their own paper.

There were even subscription requests - including ones from the Library of Congress and the U.S. Air Force Academy!*

With Steve and I putting in 8 and 10 hour shifts every night after we'd finished our day jobs for the Marine

---

* How in Heaven's name can one claim to be running a respectable revolution when the Library of Congress and the U.S. Air Force Academy are asking to join your mailing list?

Corps, we started making sense of it, but there was just so much to do: We needed more contacts on the three bases around us. We needed to publish another edition of the paper. We needed more articles and artwork. We needed to answer all those letters and figure out what the heck we were doing. In the midst of that a minor crisis developed in the form of our needing to renew the rental of the PO Box. Somebody's name needed to go on the application, and whoever it was would be "outed" as clearly connected with the paper. It needed to happen, and no one else seemed willing, so I sucked it in, and went down to the Post Office and did it.

We also discovered, much to our surprise and delight, that our little home away from home in Swansboro was a way station on the anti-Vietnam military desertion underground railroad. We found this out when a guy with a short haircut showed up unannounced one day and suggested that he'd been told that we might be able to help him get "north" - meaning ultimately Canada. He was Army, from some base in Georgia or Florida - we didn't press him for details or even for his name - and had made contact with an anti-war group there who had helped him get as far as us with the understanding that we would cover the next link. We made a few calls and found someone who was headed up to Washington, DC who was cool about taking him along and dropping him off to some people there who affirmed they'd get him to New York.

A number of people came though that way during the summer, and only once did that give us pause: We were at the apartment just doing all our normal stuff, Steve and I working like maniacs, everyone else smoking the demon weed or whatever, when we heard car doors slamming and then a very purposeful set of footfalls coming up the wooden stairs, which turned out to belong to two guys in black suits.

They gazed in the screen door, and then simply asked this guy who'd recently wandered in on one of those northern journeys, "Are you so-and so (his name)?" He responded, "Yes I am." They asked, "Will you come with us?" And he responded, "Yes I will." and got up and left with them, with the rest of us not saying another word, or moving, or breathing, or having any heartbeats, or anything else! We never heard another word about him or the incident, which was pretty incredible because there were enough drugs laying around to put us all away forever, and they (the guys in the suits) had to know who and what we were - not to mention the fact that we were clearly "aiding and abetting" someone who was deserting. But oh well! We got a free one that time!

In addition to our work directly on and with the newspaper, we all did a lot of posting of anti-war posters, "how to desert" pamphlets, notices of impending demonstrations, etc. on bulletin boards on base, planting marijuana seeds in the flower beds at the Commanding General's house, and such other random acts of psycho-rebellion as came to mind.

The other big thing of note - something I am very proud to have been part of - is our picking up on something alluded to in one of the piles of papers I went through out at the apartment. One of the original staff had been looking into a phenomenon we too had noticed: Cherry Point, where most people were pilots, aircraft mechanics, air traffic controllers, and a host of other occupational specialties that required a lot of training and might lead to good civilian jobs, was disconcertingly white, while Camp Lejeune where most people were basic grunts (Marine for "infantrymen") who got little training, were most likely to get killed, and would leave the Marine Corps with few skills of use in finding or keeping civilian jobs, was disconcertingly black. Going from the one base to the other was like going from Europe to Africa.

The interesting thing was that we had all taken a lot of tests in boot camp and had supposedly been assigned training and occupational specialties according to our test results. Was it really statistically probable for white guys to almost universally test positive for good jobs and black guys to almost universally test positive for shitty jobs? We had our doubts, so we started poking into that, checking peoples' test scores, and you have never seen any pattern as clear as the one our research revealed. The ONLY thing that mattered was race - white guys went one way, black guys went the other.

President Truman had issued an Executive Order ordering the U.S. armed forces to end racial discrimination in 1948, but the Marine Corps was so dominated by career officers and NCOs from the states that had comprised the Confederacy [there still weren't many job opportunities for them "back home"] that it had dragged its feet as much as possible in changing how it integrated itself. That totally offended my sense of right and wrong, because if someone made it through Marine Corps boot camp, they had earned the right to be treated with respect and to be treated fairly by the Marine Corps.

In practical terms, among the 1,001 things that were wrong about the sort of racial discrimination the Marine Corps was obviously still engaging in was that it made it pretty likely that someone you might need to depend on in a combat situation had NOT been placed in their role as a result of their having an aptitude for it. That was an excellent and very stupid and unnecessary way to get a lot of extra people hurt or killed.

Fortunately, at about the time we were finalizing our research and documentation, there was a big race riot at Camp Lejeune, and some members of Congress took an interest in the possibility that the Marine Corps might have a race problem. Our stuff found its way to them, and they went ballistic. They called the Commandant of the Marine Corps on the carpet and demanded immediate reform of the Marine Corps testing/training/job assigning policies and procedures. The Commandant complied, but he didn't seem too happy about it. We figured that sooner or later we'd get ours as a result, but we didn't care. We'd struck an effective blow for human rights - our/my little piece of the Civil Rights movement!

Our equipment in Swansboro was limited to three or four manual typewriters, so the printing of the paper had to be done elsewhere. From the piles of papers I sifted through I patched together that the founding group had supposed they would link with the American Servicemen's Union in New York which was a labor union an Army guy (quickly ex-Army guy!) by the name of Andy Stapp was trying to get started. Andy is a hero, but also was a jerk: If you were going to run off your paper on his press, he wanted veto authority over what you printed, and it had to toe his party line (he was a control-freak Socialist). I'm not sure if our guys ever did work with him, but eventually they found a good available press in the basement of the joint headquarters of SDS (Students for a Democratic Society) and the Black Panther Party in Washington, DC.

The deal was that we would put together our paper on lay-out sheets, take them up to Washington on a weekend pass, use the press to run them off, and bring the printed copies of the paper back with us. It was great fun; we'd walk in unannounced and tell whoever was watching the door that we were Marines working on overthrowing the government and could we please use their printing press to run off our newspaper? They'd freak!

This arrangement worked well except once - which coincidentally ended up being our last trip up there - when we arrived only to find the placed deserted and locked up! That was no good, since with weekend passes we had a pretty narrow window to get the paper run off! While pondering the finer points of breaking and entering, we started doing our final typing and layout work out on the sidewalk. It was late at night in the middle of a very rough and predominantly black neighborhood, and the pimps, ladies of the night, drug dealers, and the occasional D.C.P.D. squad car who wandered by seemed mystified by the spectacle of four white guys with short haircuts setting up a newspaper production office under a streetlight.

Around dawn a carload of the people who normally worked at the building showed up with a key. They were all blathering on (they seemed to be under the influence of some illegal chemical substances) about a place they had tried to get to called "Woodstock" where there was apparently a big music thing of some sort going on. We said, "Yes, yes, to hell with it: We need to get this paper out!" and took over the basement, for the first time running the big presses ourselves, figuring out how to do it as we went along.

When we returned to Swansboro, we found that over the weekend our apartment had been broken into, and that while drugs, money, postage stamps, etc. had not been touched, things like mailing lists, correspondence, etc. were gone. Among the missing items was a set of notes I had made to help me keep track of who was who in my reading of Bertrand Russell's *The History of Western Philosophy*. I was into the early Greeks at the time and had had a hell of a time keeping track of them, thus the notes, which showed up years later in my Naval Intelligence file. I always hoped that they (the N.I.S. people) had spent many hours trying to break the code I must have been using with all the strange names and concepts! Bastards. I never could bring myself to start reading the book over again.

Normally we would bring the papers onto base for distribution under our clothes. It would have been lots easier in the winter, but even in the summer I could rubber band or tape dozens of copies to my legs and torso and then hitchhike onto base, ideally with an officer (Marine pilots are not as fussy about picking up enlisted people as most officers) so there was less chance of getting searched at the gate. Once on the base, we would wander around leaving copies here, there and everywhere. For example, one of us might go see a movie at the base theater and change seats 20 times during the film, leaving a copy behind each time.

Unfortunately this time somebody got greedy and tried to smuggle the whole load onto base in the trunk of their car. The authorities somehow got wind of it, and with us watching out the barracks window, they pried open the trunk with a crow bar and busted him. Another of us got busted shortly after for something else. Then Steve got rush orders for Vietnam.

Of particular concern was something they did to a guy we were working with at Camp Lejeune: Simon something-or-other. He was black, and Black Power/Black Unity was all the rage at the time, with special, very elaborate handshakes, etc. Anyway, out of the clear blue he got a call from another Brother saying he was in trouble and needed Simon's help and would Simon please meet him over in the entrance of the bowling alley in a few minutes?

Simon said it smelled funny, but he went anyway. When he got there, the guy said he'd heard that Simon sold heroin, and could he buy some from him please? Simon quickly set him straight that he'd heard wrong, that Simon didn't have anything to do with drugs (which was true). The guy was acting all kinds of nervous and weird, and quickly thanked Simon anyway, and darted out the door and around out of sight. Simon said he stood there a second pondering what the heck had just happened, when he suddenly found himself surrounded by MP's and being frisked. When they didn't find anything on him, they hustled him out and around out of sight of the doorway, out of which an MP emerged a minute or two later victoriously carrying a little plastic bag containing some kind of white powder (later identified as heroin) which an observer with binoculars up on the roof of a building across the way said he'd seen Simon hide under the carpet.

Simon was court martialed, and despite the fact that his defense attorney took the Court up onto the roof of that building across the way at the same time of day and showed how sun glare on the glass made seeing in impossible, at which point the binocular person admitted he'd lied, and the fact that their were no fingerprints or any other evidence linking Simon to the plastic bag, they convicted him and sentenced him to eight years at hard labor and a dishonorable discharge. At that point we started getting a little fatalistic. We knew we were doomed, but we were determined to go down fighting.

One day a group of us were holding an informal meeting out on the lawn on base, laying around trying to look like a bunch of people just lying around, but talking seriously about what the heck was going on, when one of the group said, "Don't anyone react - just be cool - but there are two people on the roof of the post office watching us with binoculars." That set off some quiet moans of laughter and "You've got to be kidding me...!", and over the next several minutes we all found itches or other excuses to glance in that direction. And indeed there they were, clearly watching us. So the question became, "What should we do?" At which point one of the group instantly affirmed, "There is no question about what we should do. We are Marines! We will attack!"

This set everyone to laughing with various references to "crazymotherfucker", etc., which did nothing to dissuade our self-appointed attack leader who said "On the count of three!" and proceeded to count, "One! Two! Three!" ...At which point we all jumped to our feet and ran screaming "KILL!" toward the post office, which was two or three blocks away. The binoculars gave a jump and disappeared. As we came sprinting around the side of the building a black Naval Intelligence car peeled off in the opposite direction.

Another time we were headed out to Swansboro in somebody's old beat-up station wagon when we realized that a similar black car was following us. We quickly decided on a plan of action: Our car speeded up to as fast as it would go, tearing up the North Carolina back roads, getting a little lead on the bad guys. Then, after we'd just barely made it around a sharp curve in the road, we screeched to a stop, and all jumped out with the cameras we had littering the car. As the bad guys came around the corner, they saw us standing there happily clicking our cameras at them and waving and cheering, which caused them (the two Intelligence people in the car) to dive beneath the dashboard and go careening by at probably 80 miles an hour with no one at the controls. That ended their chasing us.

My Naval Intelligence file later revealed that at about the same time they were periodically searching my locker and were finding things (documents, buttons, etc.) which said evil things such as "Stop the War!". But I'm no fool, so I never kept much of anything there. Why would I? I had a security clearance and I worked in a security area (I was by then back to working in the communications center), which is where lots of secrets are kept safe from snooping eyes, so that is where I kept everything.

Day-to-day on base, I was a model Marine. My shoes were always shined, my hair was short, I did a snappy salute, I passed all inspections, and I did my work well. That seemed to me like a smart way to put some distance between my immediate superiors and the intelligence people I knew were out to get us. I figured that having a schizophrenic record ("He's good!" "No, he's bad!") couldn't hurt. On everything that really didn't matter, I gave the Marine Corps 110%. The other 10-12 hours a day were mine - and The Revolution's!

That summer and fall were simply insane, so if this account of them seems jumbled, it accurately captures the spirit of the times. North Carolina weather was mostly hot and humid, but it did produce one surprise while I was there: I reported out for a communications center watch one stormy day and found the place full of C-rations and other survival gear, with everyone but the comm center staff pulling out, back to high ground, leaving us behind with orders to "man the fort", and the assurance that they'd all come back "as soon as it was safe". Meaning what? Hello? Do you guys know something we should know? And who exactly decided we should stay while you all go? Etc. Etc.

But stay we did, and fairly quickly the wind started picking up and things started blowing all over the place, and we found that if we unbuttoned our shirts and held our shirttails out like wings and leaned into it we could occasionally lift off the ground like flying squirrels! But then it started raining like hell, which was less fun. The hurricane, which was a big one I understand, did indeed touch the coast right there where we were, but then bounced off it and went away. So all we had was an extended watch with nobody around to bother us.

Another surprise was something that began innocently enough out at Swansboro but which came closer than anything else did to blowing apart our little group of budding revolutionaries: Steve and I were working like maniacs on the paper as usual, with other people chipping in articles or cartoons, etc. occasionally, and something was said about how the U.S. had just landed people on the moon. Steve or I, I forget which, said something to the effect of "big deal...", and someone took offense, and before we knew it people were taking sides and we nearly had a riot of our own on our hands!

No amount of mollifying would get the "the moon landing IS a big deal" side to back off and shut up and let us get back to the business of trying to stop the war. I was amazed at how serious people were about it, but in retrospect it was probably a pretty good indication of just how patriotic a group we were. Some of those guys had tears of pride in their eyes over the U.S. accomplishment; these were guys doomed to be court martialed and otherwise abused by the government, and yet were willing to punch anyone who cast aspersions on the significance of the U.S. moon landing. Go figure! Steve and I were into stopping the war, period.

One thing in North Carolina that did prove useful was a class I got to take somewhere in the midst of my time there in "Electronic Counter-Counter Measures" which is what to do if you suspect somebody talking on your radio network is one of the bad guys pretending to be a good guy, how to get around jamming, etc., all with the sort of field radios used by troops in the field in Vietnam. I am not sure how much I learned about all the cloak and dagger stuff - what to do if they know that you know that they know that you know - but I did appreciate having a week to be a radioman and learn all about the radio and how to use it more thoroughly than we'd been taught in Comm School back in San Diego. Since it was common knowledge that most of us "communicators" were going to end up carrying radios in Vietnam I figured knowing how to use the darned thing couldn't hurt!

There had been some major battles in Vietnam that hadn't gone particularly well and the anti-war movement was picking up a lot of steam looking toward some major demonstrations in the fall. People were getting busted, kicked out, jailed, or sent to Vietnam all around me, while race relations in the armed forces in North Carolina went straight to hell in a handbasket, culminating in a series of race riots on all the major bases and even on ships off the coast.

Things were especially weird during the race riots. To keep our capacity for violence to a minimum, they made us all turn in our rifles and bayonets, so when we drilled we had to pretend to have rifles! Who needs drugs to feel like the world is slightly loopy?

Because I was so conscientious about sending people at other bases information on how to start and run a paper* and getting people in touch with one another and getting GI papers talking with one another, etc., I had become more or less the coordinating entity for the entire worldwide GI press movement. This was a bad situation, because I knew that I could be busted at any moment.

I successfully begged the people at the Student Mobilization Committee (later named "New Mobe") to take over that role, and shipped many of our files, contacts, etc. to them. But when *Win Magazine* of the War Resisters League decided it wanted to run an article on how to organize and run a GI paper, New Mobe referred them back to me. So out at work - in my secure workspace - I wrote the article they ended up using in their December 1969 edition. The Underground Press Syndicate and/or the Liberation News Service circulated it, and it was widely reprinted, becoming the definitive "how to" guide for GI papers everywhere.

I'd also begun corresponding with a group in the L.A. area of California called "Individuals Against the

---

* Not that we were so successful that our paper should necessarily have been the model that other people aspired to copy!

Crime of Silence" which was trying to get people to sign statements of conscience against the Vietnam War. The idea was that those would somehow be communicated to the United Nations, which might then find a way to bring an end to the war. I thought it would be cool to involve GIs in that effort, but I'll come back to them later.

Things had begun moving very quickly. Our apartment had been burglarized, we knew we were being followed, we knew they knew who we were, most of our papers had been confiscated from the car trunk, Steve had been shipped out... and I was pissed off! Take our damn papers will you?!? Think you've shut us down, do you?!? I got on the phone and called the SDS/Black Panther folks in D.C. to see if they still had the printer plates from the paper. They did, so I asked them to run 500 more copies and send them to me. They said they could and would... if I could come up with the money to pay for it, since they were in the middle of one of their periodic revolutions within the revolution, and were more or less under siege by whichever side had been declared counter-revolutionary and had been locked out.

So now I needed funding. There was a group in Boston that seemed promising: The U.S. Servicemen's Fund. They were an anti-war group, and the name certainly suggested money. I called and talked to the guy running it,* who cautioned me that I was doomed, but readily agreed to wire the needed money to D.C. The people there said they would print the papers and send them down to me at Cherry Point on a Greyhound Bus.

The next morning I reported into work, only to be told that I had to go over to the Squadron Office for

---

* I believe his name was Robert Zevin.

something or other, which was not good. Having to go there was never good, because it meant that something was about to happen to you, which in my case was not likely to be anything I would want, but I had to go anyway. I walked in and identified myself and this ugly and most unfriendly Master Sergeant looked up and snarled, "How soon can you leave?"

"I only just got here!" turned out to be the wrong response, so I asked, "Where am I going?" He flipped a piece of paper that was on his desk around so I could read it. It turned out to be orders from Headquarters, USMC, directing Pfc J. M. Arnold, 2498679, to report for duty, post haste, to "the Fleet Marine Force Pacific, Western Pacific, Ground Forces", which was Marine Corps-speak for Vietnam Infantry.

There it was. What I had enlisted for. I have to admit that seeing it in black and white was a breathtaking experience. Gulp! Danged if they hadn't gone and called my bluff!

This posed an immediate problem, because I had a big box of newspapers addressed to me on its way to Cherry Point. If I left town before that arrived, it could fall into the wrong hands and all manner of bad things could arise from it, not to mention the papers being wasted!

Mentally crossing my fingers, I told the Master Sergeant that I had clothes at the cleaners that wouldn't be done for three days and so couldn't possibly leave before then. He bought it, so I had the time I thought would do the trick, until the next day when I checked in with Greyhound for the 27th time and they told me that the box had been accidentally shipped to Camp Lejeune and that it would take "several days" to get it back. At this point I threw a fit, stomping up and down and pounding on the counter demanding satisfaction, figuring that being considered an unreasonable jerk was the least of my worries. Eventually they gave in and sent a jeep to go get it for me.

They delivered the box directly to me at my barracks, which was a pain because when you get a package everyone naturally wants to know if it is cookies from home, etc., and it would be pretty awkward to explain, "No, it is just revolutionary pamphlets calling for the overthrow of the government and that sort of thing..." I stuffed my locker full of papers and began a marathon distribution campaign, ultimately distributing every one of them.

I also made a final trip out to Swansboro to get a feel for the lay of the land there. Since no one seemed to have a clue about continuing the paper (although someone eventually did pick it up again), I decided that leaving all kinds of incriminating stuff lying around was probably not a good idea, so I packed everything up and mailed it to myself at my folks' house in California, and closed the Post Office Box, forwarding that mail there as well.

With everything tidied up, I packed up my gear and went over to the Squadron Office to pick up my Service Record Book and transfer orders. I was astounded to be handed, along with those, orders promoting me to Lance Corporal! Not only was I being promoted, I was being promoted "meritoriously" because of what a good fellow I had been! There was not a hint in any of it that I'd ever been anything but a model Marine: My "Secret" security clearance was intact, and they were sending me off to handle all kinds of classified material in a war I was obviously committed to trying to stop. It was very strange, but if it was okay with them, it was fine with me!

Chapter Five
On the road to "Over There"

I flew from North Carolina back to Michigan, mostly to say good-bye to my dad's dad who was dying of cancer and almost certainly would not survive my year overseas, then on to L.A. where my folks lived. My Naval Intelligence file later revealed that they either had someone tailing me that whole way, or had people at the different points checking on me, apparently for fear that I would bolt to Canada or do something else they didn't want me to do. Your tax dollars at work!

They had to give you 30 days leave before sending you overseas, so I had a little time on my hands and tried to use it productively. I wrote lots of letters, wrapping up leftover Head-On!/Wish correspondence, and beginning a tradition that I kept going for many years, which was starting at the beginning of an alphabetical listing of Members of Congress (torn out of an Almanac) and writing letters to each and every one of them asking them to stop the war. When I got to the bottom of the list, I would go back and start at the top again. I put a hash mark next to each Senator or Representative's name each time I wrote to them; by the time I left Vietnam I had written to each of them seven times.

I ran over to the office of the Individuals Against the Crime of Silence and together we put out a mailing to all GI newspapers (there were over a hundred of them by then) asking them to join in the effort to make GIs a significant part of petitioning to stop the war. I may also have put the finishing touches on the "How to Start and Run a GI Newspaper" article for WIN magazine during that time.

In addition to writing letters, I attended huge peace rallies at UCLA and USC, in uniform, urging people to "Support our Troops by Bringing them Home!" People freaked out when they heard what I was up to: That I really was a Marine, and that I really was going to Vietnam to work on stopping the war from the inside over there. At both places I set up a card table with a display of GI newspapers, and lots of the Individuals Against the Crime of Silence petitions. During the brief moment a year later in Vietnam when I saw my Naval Intelligence file, there were several 8-1/2 x 11 glossy photographs of me standing behind my little table, just like Arlo Guthrie's trash in "Alice's Restaurant". Too bad those got lost - more on that later.

The big rally at USC was in the evening, and concluded with a lovely ceremony in a big outdoor pavilion. They had handed out candles in little paper holders, and after it got dark they turned out all the lights and while everyone was singing some appropriate song ("Let There Be Peace On Earth"?) they lit a candle over in one corner and then used it to light two more, who then lit two more, etc., so that eventually this wave of lightings swept through the crowd, and for a few shining moments one really did feel like there was hope for humankind. It was truly one of the most moving moments of my life.

When the rally broke up, I hopped in the little sports car my brother had left behind when he got posted to Alaska in the Coast Guard and headed back to the freeway to go home. Right by the entrance ramp there was a guy covered with buttons (as we all were) still holding his burning candle, with his thumb out. I pulled over, he jumped in and off we went - for about 300 yards before a distinctive blue flashing light behind us suggested that we should pull over.

The California Highway Patrol officer was actually chuckling when he walked up to the side of my car - where I and the other guy were busily ditching buttons as fast as we could. He said he bet that I didn't know why he'd pulled me over? I admitted he was right. He then rattled off more offenses than I can even recall: I had pulled over to pick up the hitchhiker without signaling, I had stopped where you cannot stop, I had picked up a hitchhiker where you can't pick up hitchhikers, I had then pulled back into the traffic lane without signaling, and had turned onto the freeway also without signaling (I seemed to have a thing about not signaling in that car!), while the hitchhiker's knee had apparently hit the button and turned off my headlights so I had been driving at night with no headlights (but was still under the entrance/exit lights and so hadn't noticed yet), etc. I held out my wrists and invited him to take me away. He said he'd settle for my driver's license.

When he saw that it was from Michigan and that I had very short hair (not fashionable at all at the time!) he asked what had brought me to sunny Southern California? I said I was "more or less passing through". "To...?" he asked. "Does the song 'Over There' mean anything to you?" I countered. "Really?" he asked. "'Fraid so," I admitted, "I report to the Staging Battalion at Camp Pendleton day after tomorrow..."

He nodded, handed me back my license, and said,

"Take care of yourself..." Very nice. I really appreciated it. Of course this all totally freaked out my hitchhiker, who had no idea who or what he had jumped into a car with, but hey, that is half the fun of hitchhiking!

Staging Battalion was where it really became clear to me that my worst fears about Vietnam were going to be proven true. Ideally the two or three weeks you spend in the Battalion are supposed to be a refresher course in basic infantry weapons, tactics, etc. as well as a bit of folklore about where one is going to be going. And indeed we did fire all the sorts of weapons once or twice, hike all over the place, and otherwise play soldier a lot, but two things really jumped out at me:

The first was that we were doomed. It became very clear very quickly that this training was way way way too little way way way too late, and that many more of us were going to die than would have been the case if the Marine Corps had just invested a little more time and energy into properly and adequately training us. For example, the very last exercise we did before departure was walking a simulated Vietnam patrol for the first time, complete with snipers, ambushes and booby traps. We all died about 20 times, and the next day we were supposed to be upbeat about getting on an airplane and going off to do that same sort of thing in a place where you don't get to get up and try again after you get "killed". I would really have liked to practice walking such patrols until I could get through at least one without getting killed before doing it for real!

Once again I felt that I and my fellow cannon fodder had been betrayed. For all the B.S. in the media about how well prepared, equipped, etc. we were, we were the walking dead, because our training was totally inadequate. I am still mad as hell about that these 40 years later. Soldiers should never be sent into war that poorly prepared.

The second thing that jumped out at me was that the war itself was doomed. In theory, the U.S. was in Vietnam in partnership with our allies the Vietnamese people trying to defend them against cruel invaders. In reality, most U.S. troops had nothing but utter contempt for the Vietnamese people, and if that wasn't true before Staging Battalion, it almost certainly was afterwards. All the trainers were Vietnam vets who were just waiting to get out (to be discharged), and every single one went out of his way to heap contempt on the Vietnamese Army, people, and culture.

Even the classes that were supposed to inspire us to treat "our allies" with respect and prisoners according to the Geneva Convention quickly degenerated into direct or indirect enticements about how much fun it was to kill, rape, murder, torture, etc. Since the Vietnamese didn't look or talk like us, and often weren't even Christians, they obviously didn't care about being killed, raped, tortured, and so on. Why, it was silly to even think about their having feelings, or caring about their families, their property, their dignity - they were "gooks" forchristsake, not people. It was almost like going out varmint shooting - and the more of them that were dead, the better! If we heard it once we heard it a thousand times: "The only good gook is a dead gook!" Lovely. Our allies.

If our troops went over there with that attitude then the war was lost no matter what else happened. And it certainly appeared that everything possible was being done to make sure that our troops were going to go over there with exactly that attitude.

The only other thing of note at Staging was the part where we supposedly learned how to throw a hand grenade. They had a guy talk about them for a while, about how all the movie scenes notwithstanding you CANNOT pull the pin with your teeth, and that conversely you should NOT straighten out the pin so that you can more easily pull it, because the easier it is for you to pull it the easier it is for a bush to snag and pull it out and blow you up, etc., etc.

Then they had us line up on a range to try throwing one. As the people ahead of me threw theirs, I noticed that the guy who was supervising would perch up on the edge of the little bunker and watch as the grenades exploded. When it was my turn I explained to him that I had never been very good at throwing things and that he might want to stay down in the bunker this time. He gave me a ration of shit about "just throw the fuckin' thing out there into the target area and cut the crap, etc., etc." I tried to explain that that was precisely the problem, that there was no way in hell that any grenade I threw was going to get anywhere near the target area which was some ridiculous distance out there. He again ordered me to "Just throw the fuckin' grenade!" So I did. And it arched gracefully up into the sky and fell with a deafening roar about 30 feet away, sending John Wayne tumbling head over heels on top of me down in the bunker cursing a blue streak about jesuschristcrazygoddamnmotherfuckeryoutryingtokillme?!

At that point in our training we knew there was nothing they could do to us that was worse than what they were already planning to do to us, so I suggested that maybe when he got his hearing back again he should start listening to people.

I don't recall if it was at Staging or before I left Cherry Point, but somewhere in the process of my heading toward Vietnam my shot card (the little passport-like booklet that all your vaccinations are recorded in) got temporarily lost, and so I had to get all the shots I had ever gotten in the Marine Corps (and there were MANY!) all over again.

As we got closer to leaving, they tightened security around us so that nobody could go over the hill. They took us out to the airport (I believe we flew out of Marine Corps Air Station El Toro) on buses like they carry prisoners in, with a cage between us and the door, and windows that don't open. Despite their precautions, I think we were all pretty much okay with the whole thing until they announced the beginning of boarding our flight just as the Peter, Paul and Mary rendition of "Leaving on a Jet Plane" started playing on the piped in music they had in the terminal. "I'm leavin' on a jet plane / Don't know when I'll be back again..." Everyone more or less lost it.

The plane was a regular commercial Pan Am flight with the normal beverage service and all. The only difference was that the only passengers were Marines going off to war. Weird. It was a long flight; we stopped over to refuel in Hawaii, and took off again for Okinawa. The only event of note during that flight was that someone in the seat behind me said that they hoped the fighting would spill over into India, because they'd always wanted to go to India. I observed that that would have to be one hell of a spillover to get that far! But he said no, it was just the next country over from Vietnam. Eventually we had him draw a map, and it turned out that he thought that Vietnam was Bangladesh! Definitely an officer candidate!

We landed in Okinawa very early in the morning. Everyone was pretty stiff and groggy. They piled our sea bags about four or five layers deep in a big line on the tarmac next to the plane as we waited for buses to come and get us. In the meantime, all the typical maintenance trucks that cluster around airplanes showed up to clean it out, fill it up, etc. The one that empties out the toilets pulled under the plane, hooked on what was probably an 8 or 9-inch hose and pushed the button or whatever to do the royal flush. Unfortunately the hose had been improperly attached to the plane, so when the flow cut loose, so did the hose - and 4,000 miles' worth of 200 Marines' deposits came spewing down onto the tarmac about 50 feet away from where our sea bags were piled!

The offending material immediately began flowing toward the sea bags, and just as immediately I began grabbing people and lining them up and barking orders as to who should throw bags to whom in which direction. In a matter of seconds I had dozens of people tossing sea bags like demons, ultimately saving every one from getting anything unpleasant on it... A big cheer went up - and then someone noticed that the organizer of the rescue effort was one of the lowest ranking people on the airplane!

I had to quickly melt into the crowd as it dawned on some of the higher ups that they had just been led in action and ordered around by someone they were supposed to be smarter, quicker, etc. than, and who they definitely outranked. Oh well! No one was more surprised than I was, however. It wasn't like it was something I'd thought about or planned. It was just a situation that required immediate action, and I took it. I hadn't expected to have those sorts of reflexes, but I took comfort in the fact that apparently

I did. It seemed like something that could prove to be an asset in the months ahead!

Afterwards, while we were standing around waiting for the buses, a flight of B-52's returned from what we assumed was a mission over Vietnam. There were five or six of them, and on Okinawa the runway goes right to the edge of the ocean at sea level. So in they came, just skimming the waves, silent, elegant, terrible. One imagines immense dragons come to destroy all that is before them, hypnotizing their victims with their beauty. It was an amazing sight.

We spent two or three days on Okinawa for no particular purpose, and then we got on another Pan Am flight for you know where. Just like on the bus to boot camp, there was a lot of bravado on this flight. A lot of people were doing a lot of tough talking to keep their nerve up, but the guy I was sitting next to was cool. He was about like me. Quiet and just wanting to get this over with.

My seatmate and I met again a month or so later at a helicopter landing zone in Da Nang when I was doing a courier run and he was on his way back to rejoin his unit after having been Medevac'd out. He had been stationed on a little hilltop base, and one night the week after he'd arrived they'd been overrun. He woke up and heard shooting, yelling, etc. and stood up just as someone tossed a grenade into the tent. It knocked him head over heels, but he managed to stand up again only to have a second grenade go off, this one blowing him through the side of the tent onto the ground outside.

With blood dripping out his ears and eyes, he'd decided that if they were going to throw grenades at him every time he stood up, then he would just refrain from standing up for a while, and crawled under the wooden floor of the tent to wait out whatever was going to come of it all. Eventually our guys pushed the bad guys out, and he'd been flown out to a hospital ship to recover. His hearing wasn't so good anymore, but in the Marine Corps who cares if a radio operator can hear!

The general bravado came to a screeching halt when the pilot cheerfully announced that the green line on the horizon was our destination, and that we should all return to our seats and fasten our seat belts for our imminent landing at Da Nang International Airport where it was a balmy 78 degrees...

Chapter Six
Arriving in Vietnam

We landed, and as we got off we were greeted with a huge cheer from the 200+ Marines who were lined up waiting to get on that same plane and fly out of Vietnam. They looked like hell warmed over, but they were very happy.

We got on deuce-and-a-half open back trucks for a ride across town to the place where they housed and processed people coming and going from country. The ride over confirmed my worst fears. We drove through one of the worst slums I have ever seen. It was abject poverty as far as the eye could see, with children begging for gum, money, cigarettes, etc. and people on the trucks dropping said items behind their truck to enjoy the spectacle of small children darting out between speeding trucks to try to snatch up those goods without being crushed to death by the next truck. Haw! Haw! Haw! What fun! Squish a kid!

Meanwhile, the drivers and guards were making obscene gestures and propositions at everything female we passed, and the drivers were obviously delighting in splashing as much mud as they could on as many people as they could. The Vietnamese, in return, radiated pure outraged hatred toward us, as well they ought. What a way to win the hearts and minds of the people!

It was only at the processing center that we all finally learned where exactly each of us was going. Until then all you knew was that you were going to Vietnam and whether you would be with the Infantry or the Air Wing. Once we got our more detailed orders - which were just the names of units - some of the people who were there waiting to leave country gathered around and were asking who we'd been assigned to?

As we answered one after another things were all pretty upbeat: "1st Marines" -- "Good deal! The 'Palace Guard' right here in Da Nang with the big PX and USO!" "23rd Engineers" -- "Oh man, some people have all the luck, right on the beach - work on a tan for me!" When it came to me and I said "5th Marines" the mood suddenly changed to pity and concern, with someone asking, "Who did you piss off?", and one after another they offered me their condolences, and in some cases a weapon of some sort "since I was going to need it." I did not find that particularly reassuring!

The 5th Marines (properly the 5th Marine Regiment of the 1st Marine Division) is the most highly decorated regiment in the Marine Corps, having stopped the big German advance on Paris in 1918 after the French and British lines gave way, and distinguished itself at Belleau Wood (where it earned for the Marine Corps the nickname "Devil Dogs"), Soissons, St. Mihiel, Blanc Mont Ridge and the Argonne. The 5th Marines had been the first to hit the beaches at Guadalcanal and had been seriously engaged in the bloody taking of New Britain, New Guinea, Peleliu and Okinawa. In Korea, they had helped turn the tide in North Korea's desperate major assault on the Pusan Perimeter at the Naktong Bulge, had been the first ashore at Inchon, and the lead regiment in the famous "attack in a different direction" that mauled multiple Chinese Divisions as the 1st Marine Division relocated from the completely surrounded and hopelessly outnumbered Choson ("Frozen Choson") Reservoir to "an amphibious landing in reverse" with all of their dead, their wounded, and their equipment at Hagaru-ri on the sea in Korea. In Vietnam elements of the Regiment had played a key role in the retaking of the Que Son Valley in 1967 and Hue City during the big Tet Offensive of 1968.

In short, the 5th Marines is a Regiment with a reputation to uphold, and an attitude. The baddest of the bad as it were - and at the time it was one of only two Marine Infantry Regiments still stationed and active out in the bush (still out in the Que Son Valley). My luck! I concede that that was exactly the sort of place I had wanted to get to all along, but wishing and getting are two quite different things!

Fairly soon thereafter they started dividing us up by assignment and shipping us out to our units on helicopters. When my turn came, about 30 of us piled onto a big double-rotor Huey and headed out west of town. They flew very high, and when they got over a base where they needed to land they flew a very tight, very steep, very fast spiral straight down, skimming the ground and pushing people out the door while the chopper itself was still moving in order to not become a sitting duck. You've seen newsreel footage of Douglas MacArthur bravely splashing to shore in the Philippines? This wasn't like that. This was more like people being pushed out of a moving car.

Eventually they got down to just the last four of us, all assigned to the 5th Marines. Where the descent to the other bases was gut wrenching, the drop into An Hoa was a chance to experience weightlessness – the helicopter dropped so far so fast we all floated about like little angels with our sea bags and papers.

As we neared the ground you could hear explosions and sirens, and this time there was no time given to niceties: As soon as we were close enough to the ground so that one could be pushed out without breaking one's neck, we were summarily pushed out into what turned out to be belly-deep bright red mud. As the chopper roared away, it coated with mud any part of us that had escaped getting covered in our jump/fall. And there we stood in a foggy drizzling rain, up to our collective asses in mud, surrounded by worn, torn walls and piles of green sand bags, rolls of barbed wire and firing cannons. Welcome to An Hoa!

We stood there for a few minutes, and since nothing had killed us yet, we decided that we might as well go try to find out where to report to in this hellish place, or at least find somewhere where the mud was not quite so deep. The former turned out to be easier than the latter. Mud was a way of life at An Hoa during the monsoons. It was everywhere, and it was so deep in so many places that eventually you just learned to ignore it. Going to the chow hall might put you in mud up to your waist. Going to guard duty could easily put you in it up to your chin. Anything that wasn't over your head was considered more or less irrelevant.

"Headquarters" turned out to be a hole in a seemingly haphazard pile of sandbags, and no one seemed at all taken aback at our being covered with mud. They pointed us in the direction of where we were to report to our specific units, and off we each went to whatever fate had in store for us.

I hadn't far to go. The Communications Company was just around the corner from Regimental Headquarters in the defensive heart of the base. I went to the Comm Office, reported in, and they summoned someone to take me to the tent they were assigning me to and "show me the ropes." Being shown "the ropes" included finally being issued jungle boots, jungle utilities (clothing), a rifle (an M-16), and all the other little odds and ends one might have assumed they would have given us at some point before dumping us smack in the middle of a war zone.

This turned out to be a hassle, because the Supply Sergeant was an asshole who seemed to delight in not giving people stuff, or at least in not giving them the right stuff. So, despite the fact that I had been wearing "Extra Small" sizes of just about everything (since I only weighed about 135 lbs. at the time), he issued me Extra Large utilities and an Extra Large flack jacket. In a time and place where "baggy" was fashionable, I would have been quite the number, but in the Marine Corps at that time and place, I was more like a turtle wearing a tent! But there seemed no point to trying to argue with him, so I took what he gave me.

"Home" was a tent about 12 feet by maybe 20 or 30 feet with a wooden floor and room enough for about 8 to 10 people and their gear. It was surrounded, as all tents were, by a blast wall of sandbags. As the new guy, I got the spot where the roof leaked.

By then it was time to eat, so my guide took me over to the chow hall. We all lined up, and as we inched closer to where the food was being served, people started pulling plates and silverware out of their clothes and pockets. When I got up to where the guy was serving he glared at me and challenged, "Well?!?" I said, "Well what?" He said, "Where's your plate?" I said that I'd rather hoped they had them, at which point I got pushed out of the way and they went on serving people who did have plates.

A kind soul who observed my plight helpfully suggested that one could go out to the garbage dumpster behind the chow hall and tear out a corner of a box and use it as a plate. So I did, eating my first meal in Vietnam - spaghetti - with my fingers from the torn corner of a box I pulled out of the garbage. A few days later someone leaving country gave me a serving spoon, and not long after I got a plate of some sort, and eventually I managed to add a fork, knife, and teaspoon to my collection. All the luxuries of home...

A few days later the Communications Officer, who turned out to be a very decent guy, observed me walking someplace and asked me about the size uniform and flack jacket I had on.* When I explained that that was what the Supply Sergeant had insisted I take, the Major suggested that he and I go and pay a call on said Supply Sergeant to see if maybe together we could do better for me.

When we walked into the supply shack, the Supply Sergeant was leaning back with his feet up on the counter, self-assured and on top of his world. Ten seconds later he was digging though his stores of goods as though pursued by the demons of hell in a frantic search for brand new "Extra Small" everything for me. I don't recall whether the Major threatened to kill him outright, or just to make him walk point (first in line, most likely to trip booby traps, get shot in ambushes, etc.) on night patrols for the rest of his tour in Vietnam, but whatever the threat was, it worked.

---

* At An Hoa one always had to wear a helmet and flack jacket when outdoors, and carry a loaded weapon, because of how often the silly place was rocketed, mortared, attacked etc. Simply being there was enough to qualify for a Combat Action Ribbon!

Or more properly, it worked until I had my first experience with the unique Vietnamese laundry system. Now, I suppose we could have washed our clothes ourselves, but that honestly never occurred to any of us, so the deal was that when you needed laundry done you took it to this place on base where some Vietnamese had this laundry business going and you turned it in, and in a few days you went back and paid them some given amount of money and they gave you someone else's clothes.

This was more or less okay, because we all were, after all, wearing pretty much the same things, but size was important. Most of the time they managed to give you clothes at least fairly similar in size to what you'd turned in, but not always. If you objected to the clothes you were given, a very curious thing would happen: All of a sudden they would lose their ability to understand or speak English. People who seconds before had been conversing in English as easily as if they'd just graduated from Harvard would suddenly be reduced to jabbering loudly and pointing in every direction and all of them would come running and everyone would be yelling and pointing and arguing with one another in Vietnamese. At that point it was easier to just take whatever they had given you and go away.

Before I could go on regular duty I had to attend a week's worth of Orientation classes out on the base's outer perimeter. My first walk out there nearly ended this tale most unceremoniously: I could see the little hut where the classes were held down this road, so I headed down the road to get there - very reasonable, yes? No.

As I got further along, the mud got deeper and deeper, going from waist high to chest high to chin high - and then I saw three tanks coming toward me down the road, each throwing a wake probably three feet high as they plowed through the mud. Thankfully there was a telephone pole just off the side of the road. I lunged to it and was able to scrabble up far enough that when the tanks went by, completely ignoring insignificant life forms such as me along the way, I was able to keep from drowning. Thereafter, I approached the hut from a different route.

"Orientation" turned out to be one of the most disheartening experiences of my life. All the bad things that had taken place in Staging Battalion were multiplied tenfold here: In Staging Battalion they had merely talked about how fun killing, torturing and abusing "gooks" is, but here they actually got to demonstrate some of it, showing us noses, ears, penises, and fingers that they'd cut off living or dead Vietnamese, bragging about the rapes they'd committed and the people they'd killed, and advising any Vietnamese who happened to be walking across the rifle range that we wanted to use it by shooting at them. Haw! Haw! Haw!

It was all so monstrously outrageous that I was numbed by it, managing only to write to my friends at the Individuals Against the Crime of Silence about what I had seen and heard, and how for God's sake they needed to double and redouble their efforts to stop this madness! They wrote back asking if there was any way that it would be okay for them to pass my letters on to the Liberation News Service so that more people could hear firsthand what was happening in Vietnam? I immediately pounced on that as a way to justify my existence and my being in that terrible place, and so began my career as an "embedded with the troops" field correspondent for the anti-war press.

My friends in L.A. were worried that publishing my

letters could "get me in trouble" but I assured them that even the Marine Corps would be hard pressed to find a more hellish punishment than stationing me where I was.

The base was rocketed almost daily. At first it was disconcerting: You'd be sitting around with some people, and suddenly they would all be gone. And then just on the edge of your sense of hearing you would begin to hear a very faint hum, which quickly grew into a shriek before the rocket slammed into the ground with a deafening explosion. After a while you learned to hear the rockets and to react to them as fast as everyone else. But then after a while longer you just said to hell with it, and let the rockets do what they needed to do without dignifying them with a lot of running around. They were going to hit where they were going to hit, and chances were pretty good that that wasn't wherever you were, and if was where you were, you were dead anyway, so to hell with them!

Of course, someone would dutifully hit the "incoming rockets" siren every time the rockets came screaming in, which was about as redundant as anything ever could be. Let's see, things are shrieking out of the sky and making loud explosions, so let's have an alarm to tell people that that is happening! And then our cannons would all start shooting back. Fortunately, the rockets almost never hit anything of consequence, although they did apparently take out the hated chow hall several times, and a warehouse full of Fanta Orange Pop at a critical moment, but I get ahead of myself.

My name was a problem: Normally in the military people are called by their rank and last name, or among people of the same or similar ranks, just by their last name. But in our small fraternity of communicators there already was someone called "Arnold" (which wasn't altogether Kosher because that was his first name, but his last name was unpronounceable), and on top of that, we also had a "John" (Pierce Benjamin John, a Navajo), so there was nothing left for me.

The situation more or less resolved itself one day when the Communication's Officer, Major Donaldson, was lugging a couple of large containers of water across the main base area to the private shower he'd built for himself.* I was empty-handed, so he hollered over and asked me to give him a hand with one of them. It was a friendly ask and not an order, and I readily agreed, but as I did so my big mouth just had to open and say something about me being "Gunga Din, faithful water boy of the 5th Marines."

The minute the words were out of my mouth his grin told me that I had just made a terrible mistake, and indeed I was never able to shake the name thereafter.**

We'll pause here to get the lay of the land: I arrived in Vietnam as a Lance Corporal "Communications Man" (Military Occupational Specialty No. 2542) on December

---

* You can tell how rustic and primitive life an An Hoa was by the fact that there was only one common shower for officers and enlisted people alike.

** When the Regimental Commander presented me with my commendation when I was leaving country many months later he read the heading, "...Meritorious Mast for Corporal John M. Arnold...," stopped, paused while looking critically at the piece of paper, and then squinted at me and asked, "Is that your real name, Gunga?"

This set all the officers gathered around to fits of giggling, causing me to chastise back, "Sir, this is an official ceremony; you are supposed to behave yourself!" which again set everyone to giggling. I admonished them (mostly Naval Academy graduates many years older and vastly outranking me) afterwards that all of my efforts to bring them up right had obviously been for naught.

5, 1969. I had been in the Marine Corps for about 14 months by then, and had celebrated my 19th birthday just a month before. At that time a tour in Vietnam was set at 365 days. I had arrived in country during the winter, the monsoon season, which meant it rained (generally pretty softly) more or less all the time for months on end, which meant adapting to knee to neck-deep bright red mud as a way of life.

I was assigned to the Communications Platoon of the 5th Marine Regiment, which had its headquarters at a place called An Hoa, 50-60 miles southwest of Da Nang. The Regiment's area of responsibility was a huge chunk of largely mountainous territory up on the Laotian border, as well as large areas along the Song Vu Gia (River), the most famous portion of which was a large, very dangerous area nicknamed "The Arizona Territory" for all the gunfights that had gone on there and because Agent Orange had turned it desert-like.

Our mission was obviously to find bad guys and do them in, but more specifically we were supposed to block what was generally considered the second main exit ramp off the Ho Chi Minh Trail, the first being further north leading toward Hue City; this one leading to Da Nang. Marine Corps Regiments have three Battalions, but the 1st Battalion was always off somewhere, so only the 2nd and 3rd Battalions had their Headquarters and many of their personnel at An Hoa. Also hanging out with us were elements of the 2nd Battalion, 11th Marines who were artillery folk with 105, 155 and 175mm guns scattered around the place, some tanks which seemed to come and go at will, and some Navy Seabees who did engineering and various demolitions sorts of things, or so I gather.

An Hoa was a big sprawling approximately triangular blob of a base that had accumulated over time and grew seemingly without rhyme or reason. There were normally at least a couple thousand people there, so as such things go it was pretty big, and well protected with many layers of defense: There was an inner ring (sandbag wall) which protected the communications center, the combat control center and stuff like that, a second ring which went around pretty much everything else, about a hundred yards of endless coils of barbed wire you had to wind your way back and forth, back and forth, back and forth through to get across, and then an outer perimeter wall of earth, which was probably 10 feet high and 10 feet across, punctuated with little defensive bunkers about every 200 feet where we stood guard duty.*

About 20-30 feet out from the earth wall was a wall of coils of barbed wire, which was probably 8 feet high and 6 feet thick, and then a big area (100 yards+ in most places) that had been bulldozed as flat and open as possible that was marked with the little triangle things that the Geneva Convention says you have to put up if there are land mines present. Clearly no one in their right mind would ever try to launch a serious attack across all of that. The most we ever seriously expected or kept watch for was an occasional sniper, or maybe an attack at one of the gates on the roads leading into the base, since the gates were the one obvious weak spot.

The main road in and out led across "Liberty Bridge" (site of a major battle in August before I got there in December) and ultimately to Da Nang, but it was rarely

---

* When I first got there they were also in the habit of staging a tank between every second bunker, down behind the berm, ready to go into action if needed.

used because it was too dangerous. Most traffic in and out came by air, generally by chopper. It was always a pain in the neck when a C-130 or other fixed-wing aircraft would land, because the NVA in the mountains around us would open up with rockets, mortars, etc. in an effort to kill it on the ground.

I have to say though, it was quite a thing to see a big lumbering C-130 land, dump all its cargo as it came down one side of the runway, turn around at the end, and immediately take off down the other side without missing a beat with rockets and shells raining down and our guns firing like mad into the mountainsides around us. I have to admire the crews of those planes; it took a lot of guts to fly into that. All the fixed wing aircraft that flew in while I was there made it back up and out again, but not all the choppers were so lucky.

Despite all that had gone on in North Carolina, my service record book indicated that I was a model Marine in good standing with a "Secret" security clearance. I figured that sooner or later my Naval Intelligence file would show up and that that would be a problem, but it hadn't yet, so my life settled into a routine of five or six general official "jobs":

The first job was working 12 hours on/12 hours off watches with a couple other people in the Regiment's underground communications (teletype) center, sending and receiving messages of varying degrees of importance. I was the one person they had whose typing was fast and accurate enough that I was authorized to transmit "live" to the world instead of typing stuff onto paper tape, proofing it, and then transmitting it; so often I was called in to be involved when something big was going on.

Other than trying to keep from getting electrocuted while working on electronic gear in ankle-deep water and dealing with the incredible bugs that would occasionally crawl out of the walls, the most interesting part of being in the comm center was seeing how events I had firsthand or at least reliable secondhand knowledge of got reported to the world. It was generally like three distinctly different events: What actually happened, what we reported happened, and then what got fed to the media and they reported.

In the latter version we were white knights in shining armor who were handily winning the war by smiting massive numbers of the evil enemy. The middle version tried to make the best of things and generally left out any unpleasantness (like the fact that the "enemy killed in action" numbers might include numerous infants, etc.). And the reality was that we were in a very dangerous place where many very bad things happened.

My second job was working over in the Communications Office, much as I had in North Carolina, but for some really delightful people this time. I loved those guys: Major Donaldson for the first half of my time there, and Major Shroyer for the second half. They were wonderful people to work with. They both knew of my opposition to the war, and both were just fine with it, to the point that I think they really liked having someone around who said things they felt but didn't think they should say.

Under Major Shroyer our office became a hangout for other Field Grade officers (Majors, Lt. Colonels, & the Regimental C.O.) who would come over to mooch coffee and to complain about how it tasted and chat about things, those things often being the various "counterculture" periodicals (the Los Angles Free Press, the East Village

Other, etc.) I would have laying around. It turns out that none of them believed the war was being won or could be won. Only the Regiment's second in command, a very constipated lifer who never hung out with us still apparently believed we were "winning".

Like any good Marine, I also had to stand 12 hours on/12 hours off tours of guard duty on the outer base perimeter. You'd go out there to spend the night, four people per bunker, lugging your own personal weapon(s) plus a radio, an M-60 machine gun with lots of belts of ammo (which made us look ever so much like Pancho Villa), an M-79 grenade launcher (commonly called "a blooper"), a night-vision scope, and lots of hand-held pop-flares. The deal was that at any given moment two people were supposed to be awake/alert/watching/etc. while the other two slept. While we did observe the two awake/two sleeping rule, the awake people often wrote letters, read, etc. by moonlight.

Occasionally guard duty would involve being part of a team of four who would be sent a couple hundred yards out in front of the perimeter to serve as a "listening post" - essentially a suicidal early-warning system. I did that probably 15-20 times over the course of the year because it was more pleasant than manning a perimeter bunker, though it did entail making our way across what was indicated on the maps as a mine field in the dark both going out and coming back. On nights when all the other people had wives or serious girlfriends back home, I'd give the radio to someone else to carry, and walk "point" (first in line) just in case.

My fourth job was making courier runs between our base and the Divisional Headquarters in Da Nang. That meant carrying a big leather satchel of written messages to Division, and then carrying one back. Initially we did all of those by chopper, but as the roads dried out when the monsoons ended we did a fair number over the road, so I got to be a jeep driver as well.

My favorite task, however, was serving as the radio operator for our base's Medical Civic Action Platoon (MedCap for short) which consisted of some Navy Medical Corpsmen, some guards, several Vietnamese interpreters, a truck driver, sometimes a doctor, and me with the radio, riding off into the wild blue yonder on a deuce-and-a-half open-back truck to offer free medical care to anyone who needed it out in the villages we visited.

We had a more or less regular route, which included our visiting many villages that regular troops would have had to fight their way into. But the other side was very cool about it - they knew medical care was needed, that there wasn't anything available but us, and that we posed no threat to anyone. If they had something going on and wanted us to skip a village, they would just fire a few symbolic tracer rounds over the bow of our truck as we approached. We would fire a few rounds back (being careful not to hit anyone!) so that everyone could save face in the matter, and then we'd just go on to the next village on our route. Often I would do the honors of the return fire with the old French Tommy gun I carried (more on that later), which made a far more impressive noise than any dinky little plastic M-16.

Once we arrived in a village, we would look up the village chief and ask him if it was okay for us to set up shop for an hour or so, and if so, where, and would he please pass the word that we were there and urge people who needed help to come on over to get it. Generally it was all pretty low-key stuff, scrapes and bruises, etc., but it also wasn't at all unusual for our guys to end up delivering a baby or for us to have to call in a Medevac chopper to lift some people out - we did that once with two entire families near death (food poisoning? malaria?) that I stumbled across in one of the "strategic hamlet" (concentration camp) villages we frequented. When someone had a bullet wound, we asked no questions.

We saw a lot of infections. Seemingly no one knew about the need to keep cuts or scrapes clean, and to keep flies off of them, so relatively minor injuries often became badly infected to the point of becoming life-threatening. Much of our time (often things would get so busy that I would end up working with the Corpsmen) was spent cleaning such wounds, putting dressings on them, and trying to explain through the interpreters (who depressingly often proved to be real jerks) the need to keep the wound clean and dry for a few days. The MedCap trips were how I kept my sanity.

Probably six or seven times I was loaned to one of the Battalions' infantry platoons for a quick air drop into some situation that had developed out in the bush somewhere, plus a couple of other just normal patrols out there. Fortunately nothing too dramatic came of any of those.

Other tasks and activities cropped up from time to time, but most of my time was split between those five or six jobs, as often as not with them tumbling over one another as they did the first time I made a courier run to Da Nang:

Slogging back up to the main base area at dawn after

guard duty, I was greeted by someone who congratulated me (very tongue in cheek) on being selected to do a courier run to Da Nang on a chopper leaving in a few minutes. They told me that I should take this big honking pouch of messages and get right down to the landing zone (LZ) because it wouldn't do to be late. I said you've got to be kidding, I've just come off an all-nighter in the mud on the perimeter; I'm tired, I haven't eaten, shaved, washed, etc. and I certainly don't know squat about being a courier (the subject had never come up before)! Surely there was someone else who could go? Nope. Take this and get your butt down to the LZ NOW!

I obeyed, and a chopper came by a few minutes later. I got on, and rode more or less the reverse trip as the one that had first brought me to An Hoa. At each stop a chopper crewman would write on a little chalkboard the unit whose LZ it was (choppers are so noisy that it is almost impossible to communicate verbally), and at each one some people would get off. I was supposed to go to 1st Marine Division Headquarters, so I kept waiting for that to show up on the chalkboard, but it never did. Eventually I was the last passenger, and they landed at this little no-name LZ by the ocean and indicated I should get off. I asked if this was Division Headquarters (which I knew it wasn't); they shook their heads "No" and threw me off anyway, and left.

So there I was with a 30 lb. sack of God only knows what, at a seemingly abandoned LZ by the ocean, hungry, thirsty, tired, a dirty, unshaven, stinky, muddy mess, with no money, no food or water, no radio, and not a clue how to proceed. Lovely!

After sitting around for a few minutes I realized that off to the west there was a fairly distinctive mountain (very big hill) with a bunch of official looking buildings on it, and I recalled hearing that Division Headquarters was on the eastern side of a big mountain on the west side of Da Nang. That had to be it. The problem was, I was clear over on the east side of the city.

I started walking, sticking out my thumb at any military vehicles that passed, but I could hardly blame them for not picking me up. I hated the M-16, which jams in a heartbeat if it gets wet or dirty, and we were ALWAYS wet and dirty, so instead I was carrying a very non-regulation 1940's French Tommy gun that fired big clips of .45 caliber rounds, which I could easily get since as a radioman I'd been issued a shoulder-holster .45 pistol, which I was also carrying, along with several hand grenades. I stunk, I was filthy, I hadn't shaved in days, and I was clearly right out of the bush. In Da Nang and other "rear" areas it was a different world: They wore regular uniforms, they polished their footwear, they wore rank insignia and saluted (which we did not do, as it made it too easy for snipers to identify who to shoot first), they washed and shaved. Hell, they mowed the frigging lawn! So next to all of that I was like something out of a horror movie.

But I was also extremely pissed off. After what seemed like ten miles of walking, I felt like I was about to drop dead of dehydration, exhaustion and frustration, and still no one would stop to help me. As I considered the merits of employing the Tommy gun to get a ride, someone finally stopped. He was even going to Division Headquarters, thank God! I told him my tale of woe, and he patiently explained that the LZ at Division is not called "Division", but rather "1st Recon", as it is technically within the 1st Recon Battalion's compound at the base of the mountain across the street from Division Headquarters. I could only hang my head and curse with all of my being those who could have told me that me earlier in my journey.

He dropped me off, and then began the next ordeal: Division Headquarters appeared to be splattered all the hell across the entire frigging side of the mountain. Was I supposed to schlep the stupid bag all over this place? I sat down and started going through the bag, and sure enough, I had mail addressed to all kinds of different places. #@$&}##!!!!! So I started making the rounds, sitting on the grass in front of every building to check whether I had any mail for them. People walking anywhere near me sincerely pretended to not be aware that I am there. Nobody wanted to deal with whatever the heck I was!

As I went into the offices to hand them their mail everyone was very nice. No one said a word about how I looked or smelled. Finally, at about the fifth or sixth place I stopped, someone helpfully suggested that, rather than walking around to all of the offices, I could just drop off everything at the Divisional Mail Center office at the bottom of the mountain... #@$%^&*()+{|@#@##@# $%$#!!!!!!! This was ANOTHER little detail of my task that it would have been ever so helpful for someone to have imparted to me at some earlier point in the ordeal...

So I trudged down to the Mail Center, and sure enough, they sweetly took everything and gave me a bunch of stuff to take back with me to An Hoa. I asked what my next step should be, and they directed me to an LZ next to Division (not 1st Recon) where I could hopefully get a chopper ride back out west. When I got to the LZ, they told me that there wouldn't be any more choppers that day, but that I could spend the night in some barracks they had for strays like me. It felt like my luck had finally changed - the barracks were wonderfully clean and dry; I got to sleep in a bed; and the chow hall had plates and silverware and everything! The only problem was the bag of messages; they had no place to lock it up, so I wound up eating, sleeping and even taking a shower with it.

The next morning they ordered us all to "fall in" at a morning formation of some sort, which I supposed was meant to tell us what time various choppers come and go. But no, that would be much too easy. Instead, they announced that in order to keep providing the nice housing and chow, they needed a certain percentage of travelers stay over an extra day and do all the cleaning, laundry, etc. That percentage turned out to be you, you, you, you, and you, with one of those you's happening to be me.

I flagged down the Sergeant and explained to him that while I'd love to help out, particularly because it was much cleaner and safer in Da Nang than back at An Hoa, the fact that I was a Regimental courier with 30 lbs. of classified messages in tow meant that I really needed to get back to my unit. To my amazement, he blew me off and said I had to stay. He outranked me and could technically order me to stay, but rank is supposed to come with brains, and detaining a Regimental courier carrying a pile of classified communications from Division Headquarters back to his unit in the field in the middle of a very real shooting war struck me as beyond stupid.

So I tried again - "Wait a minute, I AM a courier carrying what could possibly be important messages to a combat unit in the field!" He blew me off again, telling me that I was staying. By this point, I was seriously getting pissed off at the whole ridiculous situation: I hadn't wanted to be a stupid courier, but now I was one, and while I didn't know how time-sensitive or important my bag's contents were, it seemed to me that if the messages were important enough to send someone like me to go get them, they probably shouldn't hang around an extra day in the big city while I made beds, washed dishes, etc. for some rear-area prima donna who had probably never heard a real gun fired in anger.

So once again I tried to tell him that I really needed to go. He got in my face – at which point I clicked the safety off my Tommy gun, which just happened to be loaded and pointing at him with my finger on the trigger. It suddenly got very quiet, and people near us edged away as I informed him one last time that I was indeed getting on the first goddamn chopper that arrived, and that if I had to do it over his dead body it would be all the same to me, and then I walked backwards to the LZ with my Tommy gun at the ready. And I did get on that day's first chopper.

After that first bad experience, doing courier runs actually became quite fun. It turned out that you really could get off your chopper at 1st Recon, and stay there as well, without the hassle of them trying to make you stay over and clean. That way you could just walk across the street, do the mail drop, and have the rest of the day free to visit the big PX and USO Center at Division. It got even better once I started driving the jeep up there - I would arrive in Da Nang carrying handfuls of money and shopping lists, and return to An Hoa like Santa Claus, my jeep loaded with piles of things to make people happy.

Chapter Seven
Prelude to Death and Destruction

Okay, dear reader, fun and games are over for a while. Despite having its humorous aspects and moments, the Vietnam War was a brutal, awful thing in which many horrible things occurred. It gives me no joy to speak of those things, but if you want to understand that war and the deadly seriousness of my efforts to stop it, you need to know of that which drove me (and many other people) to such levels of commitment.

The war had effectively begun in 1939, when a coalition of Vietnamese nationalist interests called the Viet Minh attempted to overthrow French colonial rule. The Viet Minh included communists, communism having supplanted Western democracy as the champion of colonial liberation in the Twentieth Century.

Before the Viet Minh were able to make much headway against the French, Japan invaded in 1940 in collaboration with the pro-Vichy Colonial Administration and the puppet King of Vietnam, Bao Dai. Viet Minh and Allied (including Free French) forces united against the Japanese/Vichy administration, and the Viet Minh were led to believe by U.S. OSS agents that when the Japanese and Vichy forces were defeated, Vietnam would be free.

No sooner had the Viet Minh defeated the Japanese/Vichy forces in early 1945, than a restored France landed its own troops with the intention of restoring colonial rule. The French had cut a deal: They could reclaim their Indochina colonies in exchange for letting the U.S. recreate a German army as a buffer against the Russians in Europe. An uneasy truce left the Viet Minh in control of the northern half of the country, but as French forces sought to supplant the Viet Minh administration in the south, often killing or imprisoning Viet Minh leaders, fighting erupted again.

The U.S. was worried about the spread of communism, and so backed the French with money, weapons, and other war materiel, giving the conflict a distinctly American flavor from the outset, even as the French reinstalled Bao Dai in an attempt to give their efforts a veneer of legitimacy.

The defeat of French forces at Dien Bien Phu in May 1954 effectively ended France's dream of retaining Vietnam as a colony. The country was temporarily partitioned, with the now openly communist Viet Minh in control of the North, and a government selected by the French and Americans headed by Ngo Dinh Diem in the South, with an understanding that elections in 1956 would unify the country.

The Eisenhower Administration's assessment was that, if the elections were held, "the George Washington of Vietnam," Ho Chi Minh, the communist leader of the North, would win. This led to a decision by the U.S. to back Diem in holding a South-only election in 1955 that preempted any possibility of reunification. As the French withdrew the last of their forces in 1956, fighting broke out between the Viet Minh and Diem's South Vietnamese Army. As Diem's and later South Vietnamese regimes' forces lost ground and popular support, the U.S. role and presence inexorably escalated until for all practical purposes it became America's war. It was a war against "communism" and not ever, not even in the most apologetic revisionist histories of it, a war for the Vietnamese people, who were seen at best as an obstacle to be worked around.

By the time I arrived in Vietnam in 1969, our side had already lost. We held some bases and cities, and controlled the sky, but it was clear that someday we would leave, that the other side would then take over, and that nothing we could do in the meantime would change that.

I wondered then, and for many years since, when exactly the tipping point was reached. When did the U.S. "lose" the Vietnam War? I believe that four books about the war taken together provide the answer to that question. They are: Frances Fitzgerald's *Fire In The Lake - the Vietnamese and the Americans in Vietnam*, Daniel Ellsberg's *SECRETS - A Memoir of Vietnam and the Pentagon Papers*, Neil Sheehan's *A Bright Shining Lie - John Paul Vann and America in Vietnam*, and, possibly most importantly, *Prelude to Tragedy - Vietnam 1960-1965* edited by Harvey Neese and John O'Donnell.

Those accounts of the years after the defeat of the Japanese lead pretty convincingly to the conclusion that enough critical errors had been made by the United States and its allies that the war was lost by sometime in 1964, the year before major U.S. combat operations began. We were fighting world communism, and Vietnam just happened to be where we were doing that. Too many of our decisions and policies focused on that objective without regard to how they impacted or were regarded by the Vietnamese people, and so they slipped slowly away like sand through our fingers, and with them any chance of victory.

No accurate accounting has ever been done, or really can ever be done, of how many Vietnamese people died or suffered wounds or other losses in their nation's 36 years of struggle, but the lowest estimate I have ever seen is a million dead* and at least three to five times that many wounded, raped, robbed, displaced, tortured or otherwise significantly injured, with most of that occurring during "the American era" from the mid-1960's through 1975.

An article in the January 1, 1973 edition of WIN Magazine overlaid the damage done in Vietnam on a map of the U.S. If what was done there had been done here on a proportionate scale, only Kentucky and Tennessee would have been unscathed. Everyone in Montana, North Dakota, Wyoming, South Dakota, Colorado, and Nebraska would have been killed. Everyone in Michigan and Indiana would have been wounded. Everyone south and west of Georgia who wasn't killed or wounded would have been made a refugee. The entire east coast would have been defoliated.

Over 3 million U.S. military personnel served on the ground, in the sky, or off the coast of Vietnam. 58,000 of them paid for that service with their lives, while another 153,000 suffered visible wounds. Many more suffered damage to their souls, minds, and for some of us, prostate glands, that did not show.

Compounding the tragedies that took and hurt so many lives, ruined so much land, and wasted so much money is the fact that most of that damage, suffering and loss occurred after the war's outcome was no longer seriously in doubt.

---

* Research reported in the June 20, 2008 on-line edition of the British Medical Journal put the Vietnam War death toll at 3.8 million persons.

Chapter 8
Death and Destruction

Prior to my joining the Marines, I had heard many stories of what certainly sounded like war crimes and crimes against humanity. But if those stories were true, those crimes were being committed by my peers, other 19 and 20-year old Americans just like me who had gone to the same sorts of schools and churches as I had. One hoped against all hope that the stories would turn out to be lies - "Commie lies" as they were often called. Stories the evil other side made up in order to discredit our Boy Scouts with guns who were trying to save Vietnam and the Vietnamese people.

But at every stage of my training my fears deepened, and the ride from the Da Nang Airport to the processing center was only the beginning of a nightmare that never ended. For the rest of that year only rarely did a day pass when I was not outraged anew by some abomination. On the bad days there could easily be a half dozen incidents. To the end, I stopped every incident I could stop, but after about six months, I started emotionally shutting down, building a very thick shell around my mind to protect it from further harm. There was simply too much too awful to endure.

There are Vietnam vets who express surprise upon hearing that the atrocities were real, affirming that "they never heard of or saw any," and I tend to believe them. There were lots of people whose placement and work (fixing trucks or airplanes at a rear base area, for example) could easily have kept them out of the loop. But I was on the radio, on the teletype, and in the loop/on the firing line virtually nonstop for 12 months, and in that year I saw and heard a lot.

What follows is "X"-rated for violent content. If you would rather not know in graphic detail what people are capable of doing to one another, please skip ahead to the next chapter. Frankly I wish I could.

Torture, murder or other mistreatment of captured persons who were supposed to be "the enemy" was commonplace. Almost every day there would be radio chatter about how none of the captives had been willing to talk until our guys had cut the ears (nose, penis, breasts, fingers, etc.) off of a couple of the other prisoners, or how they had dragged some behind a truck, or tossed a few out of a chopper over the ocean, or driven a tank slowly over a few from the feet up. People would usually be laughing as they related those incidents, and people wearing dried fingers, noses, ears, penises, etc. on chains around their neck was common.

In the book *The New Soldier*, which was published by the Vietnam Veterans Against the War, Lance Corporal David Bishop of "H" Company, 2nd Battalion, 5th Marines told the following story. I heard of a very similar incident in 1970 on the day it occurred:

"There was this operation called Meade River. ROK (Korean) Marines, ARVNs, U. S. Marines, and U.S. Army were involved. On part of the operation we had just gotten through making heavy contact and we went through a bunker system. It was a large bunker system and we found hospitals. We came across four NVA nurses that were hiding out in one of the bunkers. They were nurses, we found medical supplies on them and they had black uniforms on.

The ROK Marines came up to us and one of their officers asked if they could have the NVA nurses. They would take care of them because we were sweeping through the area and we couldn't take care of any POWs. So, instead of killing them, we handed them over to the ROK Marines. While we were still in the area the ROK Marines started tying them down to the ground. They tied their hands to the ground, they spreadeagled them; they raped all four.

There was like maybe ten or twenty ROK Marines involved. They tortured them, they sliced off their breasts, they used machetes and cut off parts of their fingers and things. When that was over, they took pop flares (which are aluminum canisters you hit with your hand; it'll shoot maybe 100-200 feet in the air)--they stuck them up their vaginas--all four of them --and they blew the top of their heads off."

In the midst of the horror, it is easy to just blow past a very telling bit of "business as usual" in that report: "...we were sweeping through the area and we couldn't take care of any POWs. So, instead of killing them..." In other words, if it was inconvenient to have them around, you could just go ahead and kill any POWs you happened to feel like killing. Try to find an okay for that way of doing things in the Geneva Conventions! Along with everything else I picked up in radio chatter and official reports were near daily accounts of POWs (which in Vietnam meant anyone who was Vietnamese who our guys decided was "the enemy") routinely being killed.

Hand in hand with the above were many incidents of wounded POWs being denied medical care. In some cases there would be some medical person who just flat out "refused to treat gooks". In other cases it might be a case of there being some wounded GIs and some wounded POWs, and the medical folk electing to work on the GIs first, which under a lot of circumstances would make sense. The trouble was that in a number of those cases our guys were only lightly wounded while the POWs were seriously hurt, and our guys even asked the medical folk to treat the POWs first, only to have the medical folk refuse.

I witnessed one such case where this Vietnamese woman was screaming in agony and the medical guy ignored her to treat some relatively minor thing on one of our guys. Our guy said he was okay, and that the Doc should go tend to the lady. The medical guy refused. Our guy got mad and insisted. The Doc refused. Our guy got up, ripped off his dressings, threw them in the medical guy's face and called him every name in the book before stomping off out of there dripping blood. I don't mean to suggest that all medical personnel over there were that way, not at all. But enough were to make you crazy.

One day I went over to the chow hall to get lunch and saw a bunch of people gathered around something someone had in a box. They were laughing and seemed to be enjoying whatever it was. So I wandered over to see what it might be. It turned out to be two female human breasts on ice. He had gotten them out on patrol and was taking them over to someone in the 2nd Battalion who in civilian life was a taxidermist who was going to tan them and make little change purses of them.

Another time out on guard duty before it got dark this very attractive young Vietnamese woman came up to the wall of barbed wire in front of us and started begging for cigarettes. I was supposed to be asleep, but was lying awake on the roof of the bunker (writing letters to Members of Congress, asking them to stop the war). The other guy who was to stand watch with me was asleep about 30 feet behind the bunker in a section of pipe to keep out of the mud.

The two guys on duty got to talking and decided that if they could entice her to try to wind her way through the coils of barbed wire far enough they could grab her. The plan then was to rape and then kill her, and after dark to throw her body back over the wire, and then to toss some grenades on it so she'd be blown up and they could triumphantly report that they'd killed someone trying to attack us ("and probably get a medal for it," one of them laughed).

They were seriously going to do that. I couldn't believe my ears. These are seemingly just normal Joes, who are about to commit rape and murder as casually as they might drink a beer.

When they went down to the wire with their packs of cigarettes and started coaxing her to come through the wire, I silently dropped down the back of the bunker, clicked off the safety on the tripod-mounted M-60 machine gun, and with my finger on the trigger and just praying for an excuse to blow those two miserable bastards away, announced that the party was over.

They were obviously completely surprised and taken aback by this new development, and quickly tried to reassure me that of course they would have offered the other two of us turns to rape her, and then when that didn't seem to do the trick, to assure me that they had only been joking about the whole thing. I assured them that I was not joking and would love to kill them if they didn't shut the fuck up and freeze. I then used such Vietnamese as I had picked up to tell the young woman to go away, as fast and as far as she could and to please never, ever, ever come back here again, because it could easily cost her life.

She did go, and when she was safely gone, I left the bunker and threw up, and just sat with my back turned to it until the Officer of the Day came around checking things, and the two conspirators told him they were worried that I was sick or crazy or something. So he relieved me from further duty that night.

Not far from An Hoa was a "strategic hamlet" that we visited in our MedCap rounds. "Strategic hamlets" were villages created out of the thin air to dry up the other side's supply and information lifelines. Essentially we would depopulate an area, forcing everyone who lived there to relocate to one of these "strategic hamlets" so that there was no longer anyone living in that area who could help the enemy with food, shelter, information, etc.

It was a very neat plan, with a few critical flaws: The biggest of which is that no people I am aware of are more riveted to wherever their ancestors are buried than are the Vietnamese. For the Vietnamese, that village is the center of the universe. It is where they must be in order to be connected to the universe. It is where the universe is kept in balance by the observance of rituals honoring the ancestors at their graves. So okay, one day we just load all the villagers onto trucks and tell them they have to live somewhere else; does anyone sense a problem?

I cannot think of anything we could have done that could have been more offensive, more outrageous, more hurtful to those villagers than making them relocate... But of course we couldn't just stop at that level of hurt; we had to compound it by making them, in their new homes, completely dependent on the honesty and integrity of the local Vietnamese government officials for their food, housing, etc., which absolutely guaranteed that they would live in abject, hopeless, grinding poverty.

One time I made the mistake of being the radioman for a small convoy running garbage from our base out to where they dumped it. I figured, how bad can a simple little run out to dump some garbage be? Two-thirds of the convoy was made up of infantrymen; and when we approached the dump area I began to understand why they were there: A cry went up and hundreds of civilians came running every direction, but particularly from the direction of the "strategic hamlet". People were pushing and shoving and crowding in as the garbage trucks tried to back up and dump their loads. The guards were shooting over people's heads and beating them away with rifle butts, tear gas grenades were thrown, it was absolute pandemonium as hundreds of men, women and children frantically scrambled for a chance to maybe find something to eat in the garbage we were dumping.

Another eye-opener was getting to visit our area's POW camp. I had to ride along to assist a wireman stringing up some new phone wire from there back to An Hoa. The camp was relatively small, housing only about maybe 20 prisoners from what I could tell. It was surrounded by all kinds of coils of barbed wire and all of that, but the heart of it was a building probably 30 feet wide and maybe 60 feet long with a tin roof, screen sides, and a wooden floor. In there were the prisoners - male, female, young, old - all standing at attention facing the screen wall. We were there for probably 90 minutes, and in that 90 minutes that is all they did, was stand at attention facing the wall. Is that what they were forced to do all day every day? God only knows. But the vision haunted me.

Out in the countryside it was open hunting season for anything Vietnamese that anyone decided they wanted to kill. Since the Viet Cong in particular were of the villages and seamlessly blended in with the general population, it sometimes was genuinely difficult to sort out who was who. But altogether too often that became license to "kill everything Vietnamese and let God sort it out!" If someone you wanted to kill (if for no other reason than you were maybe bored, or wanted to check the sights on your rifle, etc.) was Vietnamese, it was common knowledge, encouraged at Staging Battalion, in in-country Orientation, and by old timers (people who had been in-country more than 6-7 months), that any excuse, including those made up after the fact, would suffice to justify your action. All you had to do was claim they appeared to be reaching for a weapon, or that upon seeing you they started to run away, or that they were secretly signaling to someone over across the way. So you could just blow them away, and more likely than not be commended for it. People knew that, and frequently bragged about having taken advantage of it.

More officially, it was during the year I was there that Operation Phoenix was cut loose to "pacify" the countryside. What it was, of course, was a U.S. administered assassination program after which the South and Central American Death Squads of later years were patterned. Every few days the local South Vietnamese authorities would provide our Scout Sniper Platoon with a list of people to be liquidated, and guides to help our guys find those individuals, and then our guys would go out and shoot them. During the year I was there they killed over 1,000 people that way. How do I know? Two ways: First, I handled a lot of their "progress reports" at the comm center, and second, they proudly kept score on a big painting of the grim reaper they had out in front of their barracks. It said, "Never have so few done in so many!" and then reported the number of people they had killed.

Among the many very serious problems with Operation Phoenix was that if your name got put on a list, people came and killed you. The question of who got to put names on the list, and for what reasons, and who double-checked the data seemed pretty loose to me, particularly since the local South Vietnamese authorities were generally regarded as essentially an organized crime syndicate, using our snipers as their enforcers. During the year I was there, Operation Phoenix operatives attached to my Regiment assassinated an average of about three people per day, every day, all 360+ days I was there.

Then there was the village of Phu Loc Six. That is the one that nearly put me over the edge, my most painful memory of the war. Phu Loc was a village just northeast of An Hoa. Our mapmakers had numbered the hamlets that it was comprised of, and one of my favorites on our MedCap trips was hamlet number six, which was a pretty little place with very nice people.

Anyway, one day when the MedCap truck approached the hamlet we could see from afar that something was terribly wrong. People were running to and fro carrying things, but there was no happiness to it. You could smell the fear a mile away. So we stopped well short of the place and pondered the situation for a few minutes. Eventually I volunteered to walk on in alone to see what was going on.

I walked in without incident and found someone I knew who spoke enough English to be able to tell me what was happening: Apparently their hamlet had been notified that it was their turn to supply the local ARVN troops with young women for their sexual amusement. The village chief had protested that while it might be possible to find such women in large cities, there were none in his hamlet. He was told that he apparently did not understand: That he WOULD send the village's young women to service the ARVN troops or else. He had refused, and they knew the hamlet was doomed, so as many as people as possible were getting out as fast as they could with whatever they could carry. Late that night the local ARVN commander called in an artillery strike and our artillery dutifully blew away Phu Loc Six.

It isn't a happy ending to the story, but I did not shed a tear when I learned later that within a fortnight of U.S. forces pulling out of An Hoa the local villages rose up and slaughtered the ARVN outpost, sparing none.

People volunteered for guard duty on the MedCap trips for a variety of reasons, but generally because it was an easy time and place to buy drugs. I knew that, but in that time and place buying drugs was okay in the great scheme of things. All kinds of things were available in the big cities, but out where we were I never saw anything but marijuana, and since just about everyone smoked it, it really didn't matter much where and when they got it. Where I did draw the line was on any member of the MedCap crew doing anything that was going to make us enemies, hurt anyone, or just simply be stupid.

I probably often wasn't the ranking Marine on the truck, but since no one wore rank insignia it was easy to just take charge, so I did. The Navy guys appreciated having someone to run the Marine end of things, so they gave me free rein. When the team assembled, I would quickly review the ground rules with everyone: That we were going out there to make friends and help people, period, and that if anyone was not aligned with that agenda they weren't going out with us. No being stupid on the road, no being stupid in the villages.

Nonetheless, at least a dozen times I had to rein people in, as often as not at gunpoint. The biggest problem seemed to be sex. There were no American women where we were, and there was no such thing as "going to town" for the weekend or for an evening. So there we were, ten thousand 19-20 year old men who hadn't touched a woman in months, and some of us apparently just got pushed over the edge by it. Where it would show up on the MedCap trips was generally some idiot going door to door waving handfuls of money and pantomiming what he wanted to do with anyone female in the home willing to do that. Imagine your reaction if your town was being occupied by foreign troops, and one of them randomly came to your door and propositioned your mother, wife, daughter, etc. that way...

The other problem we had from time to time was with the Vietnamese interpreters (South Vietnamese Army troops who knew some English) we were stuck working with. Some of them were just bastards. Maybe you were working with some sweet little kid or some old grandmother who was just scared to death of you, but who had mustered up enough grit to come over and let you work on them, and you would want to very gently explain to them what you were doing and why, and to explain how they needed to keep the dressings clean and dry, and instead of helping with that the interpreter would yell at them and make them cry. I eventually figured out that most of the interpreters were city kids who had attended Catholic schools, which is where they learned some English. They felt nothing but contempt for and embarrassment about the very simple, generally un-educated and nearly universally Buddhist villagers we were treating.

I am seriously a gentle person, but more than once I threatened to kill one of those assholes for being mean/discourteous/frightening to one of our patients. The job wasn't all that frigging hard: Just tell the people what I've told you to tell them in a nice way, okay? It's real easy. And if you've got issues you need to work out by yelling, you work those out some other time, because the next time you yell at one of my fucking patients I am going to rip your heart out and stomp on it and is that clear enough for you, you mean-mouthed motherfucker? Damn, they made me angry. Bastards!

Patrols and convoys were textbook opportunities for people to do things right, or to do things horribly wrong, and of course what I generally observed was people doing things horribly wrong. The Vietnamese, like everyone else, are a proud people, and as a general rule they don't like to be under the thumb of foreigners. Friend to friend as equals they are as warm and friendly as any people on earth, but lord over them and they don't like it.

So when our troops were out on foot patrols or driving in convoys, it would seem pretty logical to play it cool. Just observing a few local customs and showing a bit of common courtesy was all that was required: Don't run people off the road. Don't go out of your way to run over their crops or clothing drying on the side of the road. Don't tempt their children to dash between speeding trucks for candy, coins or cigarettes. Don't shoot at people for fun. Don't shoot their livestock. Don't grope women. Don't expose yourself. Don't shout insults at people. Don't steal stuff. Don't mess with religious shrines - this was not rocket science level stuff!

But on the average patrol or convoy you would see people violating all of these simple rules and more, seemingly doing everything humanly possible to make the local people hate us. Later on I had many conversations with Viet Cong, and in every single case it turned out that they had become Viet Cong not out of a love for or even an understanding of communism, but rather to avenge some insult or injury inflicted on them or their family by some stupid American or group of Americans. That is why we were losing the war: We were creating new Viet Cong faster than we could possibly kill them!

When I drove the An Hoa-Da Nang run in a jeep, there wasn't much I could do, but a couple of times when I was manning the M-50 machine gun mounted on a deuce-and-a-half I fired or threatened to fire at trucks in our convoy who were screwing around (running over crops that were drying on the side of the road, etc.), and endangering us all.[*]

*   We were, after all, going to be returning on the same road, and the last thing on earth we needed was for everyone along the route to want to see us all dead!

One otherwise disgusting situation which did end up having a semi-happy ending caught me completely by surprise one day on base as Charlie, one of my tent-mates and best friends, and I were walking across the base (An Hoa) to pick up our laundry. We rounded a corner into what I guess was the Intelligence or Interrogation area, and found this jerk (another Marine) who was very roughly shaking a tiny old Vietnamese lady like a rag doll and screaming in her face over and over, "You Marilyn Monroe! You Marilyn Monroe!" The old lady was in absolute hysterics, and was crying in protest that she wasn't what he was accusing her of being.

It is not often that other people react faster than I do, but Charlie was way ahead of me on this one: Without a word he strode into the situation and with one blow he lifted the jerk right off the ground, sending him flying into a heap on the ground about six feet away. I caught the old lady as she fell, and both Charlie and I drew our shoulder-holster 45's and announced that fun time was over (there had been some other Marines standing around laughing and enjoying the tormenting of the old lady), and that if we ever witnessed such a scene again...

We took her down to the medical area where they often treated Vietnamese civilians and were used to getting people back to their villages. We told them that she had been badly shaken up in an accident and was pretty traumatized but probably mostly just needed to get home again. We gave her some money, not knowing what else to do to try to compensate her for what she'd been through, and left her to the medical folks.

A Vietnam vet by the name of John Beitzel was interviewed in 1971 about what he'd witnessed during his year in Vietnam. He was asked: "Did you ever witness the burning of villages, free fire zones, forced relocation of villagers, mistreatment of civilians, electrical torture, or the mutilation of dead bodies?" "Of course I did," he responded, "I was in the infantry."

In Vietnam, the futility of our efforts, the inability to tell friend from foe, the heat, the mud, the death of friends, the lack of firm control on inappropriate behavior, and the general immaturity of our troops (we were the youngest army America ever sent to war; most of us were just 19) resulted in tragedies and crimes one wouldn't have thought possible had not one been there in the midst of it. Every day the war continued was just more death and ruin. Not trying to stop the war was, for me, not an option.

Chapter Nine
Winter

It is now the winter of 1969-70; I've been in Vietnam for a month or so. I am writing up reports on what I am seeing and hearing and sending them off to the Liberation News Service via the Individuals Against the Crime of Silence folks, and I am writing massive numbers of letters to Members of Congress[*] telling them that keeping this war going is a terrible mistake. I figure that sooner or later my Naval Intelligence file is going to show up and the proverbial shit will hit the fan, but until then I am keeping busy as much as possible doing whatever I can that might contribute to trying to stop the stupid war, or at least the bad parts of it that I have direct contact with.

An Hoa was not a happy place when I got there. Almost everyone seemed to hate the Regimental Commander, who knew it, and so largely hid out in the Combat Command Bunker, which was the most heavily guarded place on the base. It was probably wise of him to stay there, because feelings were running high enough that within just a few weeks of my arrival someone tossed a hand grenade into an officers' tent about three tents over

---

[*] We got free postage to send letters back to the U.S. from Vietnam. On a slow night shift at the comm center, or out on guard duty with a full moon, I could write maybe 50 letters to Members of Congress about how they needed to stop the war. Ultimately I believe I wrote over 3,000 such letters during my 12 months in Vietnam; about 7 each to every Member of Congress. This was also probably the reason that I eventually developed an allergy to the glue on envelopes.

from mine and killed one officer and wounded several others. Much more common were tear gas grenades, which almost everyone had access to and used liberally as a joke or to just mess with people. Once I was in the Command Bunker and someone tossed a tear gas grenade in the door. Everyone freaked and went running out, abandoning the place!

There were about six radios going at the time, talking with troops in the field, choppers in the air, etc. So I sat down and managed the place until other people straggled back in wearing their gas masks. I knew that tear gas can't kill you or do any long-term harm unless you are in a very small space; it can make your eyes water only so much and make you cough only so much, and after that it is something you can work around if you put your mind to it. A month or two later I did sort of the same thing when someone gassed the Communications Office. The gas is actually a very fine powder, and as powders do, it eventually settles to the ground, but then like a powder it can be easily stirred up again. So for about two weeks after the Comm Office got gassed I was the only one who could work in there. Ah, solitude! Those were the quietest weeks I had over there.

It was at An Hoa working the radios in the Command Bunker that I had an experience that I am at a loss to describe other than to just tell the story: A call came in from five Marines who had been assigned to an ARVN Company on patrol out in the bush. They had walked into what our guys estimated was a Battalion-size ambush, and when the first bullets started flying, the ARVNs took off running. This posed a problem, because Marines do not run. And indeed our guys reported that they had already overrun two machine gun nests and were about to go after a third one. They requested direct air and artillery strikes on their position. And then the radio went dead.

While it wasn't anywhere close to that, my 15 seconds of fame came not long after, on the anniversary of the Tet Offensive, when the people running An Hoa decided to send out lots of extra patrols and listening posts to guard against any surprise attacks on the base. I was with a listening post over on the 3rd Battalion's side of things, otherwise known as "Delta Sector", and in our wandering out to where we were to spend a long, cold, miserable night laying in the mud and rain, we bumped into a much larger patrol that was supposed to go even further out and set up an ambush. They and we decided to stick together and go only about a mile out and form a big circle, with everybody facing out, and call it good.

That worked until about midnight when a stupid chopper flew over. Shortly afterwards, we noticed a step-up in activity back on base - we could see people running to and working on the guns (cannons) on the side of the base facing us - but we were obviously still pretty taken aback when white phosphorus marking rounds started landing right around us! Apparently the chopper had seen us somehow, decided that we were the enemy, and called in an artillery strike!*

Someone needed to tell those bozos that they were firing on friendlies, and they needed to do it within the

---

* When artillery fires a mission they first shoot around the edges of the target with white phosphorus rounds which go off like a giant camera flash bulb and so can be seen from miles away. When whatever artillery observer they are using confirms that they have the target bracketed, they switch to regular explosive rounds and fire to saturate the bracketed area.

next few seconds or we were all dead. But in the light of the explosions around us, I could see that the guy with the radio had frozen up; he wasn't doing anything but looking dazed. I jumped up and started to run across the circle to where he was when I heard a round coming in that had my name written all over it. It wasn't going to hit off on the perimeter somewhere, it was going to hit where I was. And so at age 19 years and 3 months, I said my good-byes as I dove to the ground, which I hit at the same instant it did, with it landing about 3 feet in front of me... a dud!

Had that shell not been a dud, this story would have ended then and there. But with no time to worry about that, I scrambled up and over to the radio, quickly switched it from the base defense frequency to the artillery frequency and called in an "All fire missions immediately cease fire!" order. I repeated it maybe three times, "This is Delta Lima Papa (Marinespeak for "Delta Sector's Listening Post"). Abort all fire missions! Abort all fire missions!"

There was obviously some confusion on the other end as to who the heck was telling them what to do, and a second or two later an officer came on demanding to know who I was and what I was doing trying to give his people orders? I could easily tell from how he was slurring his words that he was drunk. As in what else can go wrong in this miserable situation?!?

I figured I needed to get him sobered up real quick, and that being nice and respectful wasn't going to do that, so my reply was as direct to the point as it was colorful, referring to the fact that if he focused his thoughts on why 'Delta Lima Papa' might be concerned about where his cannons were shooting he might be able to figure out why the hell we would like them to stop! After a moment the firing did stop, but then they called back and wanted to know who it was that had spoken to the Artillery Officer that way? I decided it was time to switch back to the base defense radio frequency and maintain radio silence for the rest of the night.

When I left Vietnam they gave me a Regimental Commendation (in the Marine Corps called a Meritorious Mast) and put me up for a Navy Achievement Medal with Combat V, and in both write-ups they referenced how I had filed reports in timely fashion and a bunch of junk like that, but that was only because they couldn't very well say that it was for keeping the Marine Corps from accidentally blowing up 26 of its own people!

I believe it was a total of seven times when we were at An Hoa that I was temporarily assigned to one of the Platoons of either the 2nd or 3rd Battalion to be a reserve radioman while they were being dropped (delivered by helicopters) into a hot situation out in the bush someplace. Three of the times we all scrambled to the Landing Zone with whatever sort of gear we imagined might be appropriate - made necessary by the fact they never told us anything about where we might be going, what we might be doing, how long we might be out there, etc., - and after a few hours were dismissed without having gone anywhere. Once we got in the air, flew around a bit, and returned to base. Only three times did we actually land out in the bush, apparently all three times to be a blocking unit should the enemy troops who were in the area or were believed to be in the area try to go through the place where we'd been dropped.

Those were fairly gut-wrenching experiences but for mostly not the reasons one might think. There was certainly the anticipation of being dropped into a battle in progress (which we never were). There was also the possibility of being in a chopper that was shot out of the sky; that sort of thing did happen, and I regarded it as one of my least-favorite ways to possibly die. Although tracer rounds did leave the ground in our direction on two of those drops, we landed safely all three times.

What really concerned me most was that infantry platoons tended to be pretty close-knit in their own strange way; often the blacks hated the whites who hated them back, and everyone had contempt for new people, etc., but in a pinch they would fight to the death to defend one another. I wasn't a part of their circle, and worse, I wasn't even an infantryman (Infantrymen in the Marine Corps have a 03xx military occupational specialty). As a radioman, I was a 2531, but even worse, I was a reserve radioman, so I wasn't even doing anything useful; I was just there in case the radioman who was doing useful things got himself killed or wounded. So their contempt, distain, etc. for me was palpable. That was okay generally, but my biggest fear was that we might get into a war crimes situation, and that my intervening could easily pit me against this entire group of strangers who had an attitude towards me to begin with.

Fortunately, that never happened. We got safely put on the ground by our choppers, we fanned out as directed by the Platoon Leader, we faced the direction we were told to, and that was pretty much it. On two of the inserts we did take sniper fire, in one case some of it directed at me and my radio. It is an interesting feeling to know that someone out there is genuinely trying to kill you! But in that case I'd flung myself behind a wall of a rice paddy without having had a chance to gauge the depth of the water and mud in it and my stupid M-16 got wet and muddy and couldn't fire even if I wanted it to. So I just kept my head down, and other people around me did a lot of shooting into the treeline until eventually the sniper fire stopped. And then a while later we loaded back into choppers and returned to base.

Similarly, I went out on a number of small "day patrols" that didn't amount to much except to give one the experience of being out in situations which could go very badly very quickly.

The chow hall back on base was almost as dangerous, because people were getting sick from eating there all the time. C-Rations, on the other hand, while not necessarily gourmet cuisine, were quite edible and wouldn't make you sick, so they were most people's first choice. The only problem was that you couldn't draw C-rats unless you were imminently headed out to the bush - or the chow hall got blown up...

Now the deal with that second possibility, the chow hall getting blown up part, was quite interesting. We were getting rocketed by the NVA in the mountains around us almost every day, and although as a general rule they never could hit squat, they must have really zeroed in on the chow hall, because be darned if it didn't blow up about once a month, always at night when no one was there to get hurt. Every time it happened, this big cheer would go up across the base, and we'd all go back to C-rations for a week or two until they could rebuild it.

The more cynical among us suggested that the Navy Seabees stationed with us, who reportedly had access to all kinds of high explosives, had something to do with it, and that it wasn't NVA rockets at all. Some people even suggested that collections of money were being taken to encourage the Seabees to blow up the chow hall during rocket attacks, but I wouldn't know anything about that.

The Fanta Orange soda pop incident was a little less subtle: Someone in the supply chain screwed up royally and our base was sent four flatbed tractor trailer loads of Fanta Orange pop at about the same time that some wrong-way bunch of so-and-so's dumped a dead water buffalo in our water supply. With it being hot and dry as hell (this was after the monsoon season had ended), it quickly became a case of there being nothing to drink but warm Fanta Orange pop. After about a week of that, people were becoming suicidal. At the time I was doing the courier runs to Da Nang in a jeep, and when the convoy would start forming up people would come running from all directions pressing money into your hands and stuffing it into your pockets pleading for Coca-Cola, 7-Up, Root Beer - anything but @%$*# Fanta %$#@* Orange!

At the big PX in Da Nang I would back up to the door and we'd load as many cases on as the jeep could carry. I guess the deal back at An Hoa was that we weren't supposed to have as much as four truckloads of pop on hand, so until the Fanta Orange supply got reduced to some lower quantity they wouldn't ship in anything else. The collections for the Seabees on that one weren't even secret. BOOOOOOOM!!!

It was a strange life. At night we'd get rocketed, mortared, tear gassed, or some combination of the three. The tear gas was just our people screwing around. After while you usually wouldn't even bother getting out of bed for it; you'd just put your pillow over your head. My tent was pretty cool; about eight other communications people were in there. We each had a cot and a little space to call our own. A couple of guys had built a little plywood annex onto the side of it and when they rotated out, they gave it to me and my buddy Charlie. It was about as psychedelic as it could get; I don't know where they'd gotten the paint, but it was a very colorful contrast to the rest of the base.

It was generally pretty peaceful in the tent; I think we only got inspected once - an unsuccessful drug search - during the whole time we were there. That could have gone very badly, but luck in giant helpings was with me: Pretty much everyone smoked marijuana cigarettes purchased from villagers. I don't know where other people stashed theirs, but I usually kept mine at the comm center because it was a secure area that only a few people had access to. On this occasion, however, I'd made a purchase while out on guard duty, and had just carelessly tossed them in my foot locker under my cot, flopped down on the cot and covered my head with my parka because it was daylight, when the people doing the inspecting burst into both entrances to the tent. They went through everyone's stuff, including their foot lockers. I could hear all of that going on, but had the presence of mind to keep my head covered and pretend to be asleep.

When they got to me, the person in charge asked, "Who is this?" Someone said it was me and that I'd been out on guard duty. The in-charge person said, "I'm sure he's okay; let him sleep...", and I did - once I recovered from the heart-attack they'd just given me! Scares like that nipped my use of such substances in the bud. They weren't enjoyable enough to be worth that sort of risk.

The only other bit of unpleasantness was one time when a drunk came wandering in to see somebody and started leaning on the little stick things sticking up from people's cots to hold up their mosquito nets - a very important bit of survival gear as malaria was a big problem - and breaking them, which he found very funny. He was already on everyone's last nerve when he tripped over an electric wire, broke it and thought it was cool that it threw sparks all over the place when it touched some screen one guy had put up around his area. He picked up the wire and stared brushing it up and down the screen throwing sparks all over the tent, onto beds, onto ammo, onto hand grenades, onto cans of copier fluid we used for cooking. About the second time his hand and head came down from one of those brushings, his nose landed on the end of the barrel of my Tommy gun. I walked him out the door backwards and warned him never to come back.

But usually it was cool. You'd get up and eat something, and then wander over and find out what the world had in store for you that day. Communications people could end up being assigned to do almost anything – go out on patrol, go out with a larger unit on some big deal operation, work the combat control center, run into Da Nang as a courier, work the teletype center, go out on guard duty or out on a listening post, or out on a Medcap run. Things had a way of surprising you. Sometimes that was good, sometimes not.

One major entry in the "not" category was happening to be by the medical area when Medevac choppers were coming in. It didn't matter who you were or what you had thought you were doing at that point, because until everyone was off those choppers you were in the thick of it, with sirens and cannons - and sometimes NVA rockets - going off all around you as you carried people and bags full of what had been people, and held bottles of fluid they were putting into people, and lit cigarettes for people and told them they were going to be okay even when you knew they weren't. I once had to carry the body of a guy I'd been playing cards with when his platoon had been called up to get dropped by choppers in some trouble out in the bush. You had to admire the Navy medics and doctors who dealt with that every day.

More fun was insane stuff like me wandering down to the teletype center one night to get something to eat* and finding the watch crew deeply engrossed in a hot card game with a lot of money on the table and about 20 messages spilled onto the floor from the incoming teletype machines. I wandered over to see if any of them were anything interesting and found one that was this very special category of message that had a special (highly classified) name and set off bells and whistles when it came in because it pertained to something of imminent and significant military importance.

This particular message said that intelligence reports indicated that our base was about to be rocketed. I suggested to the card players that someone over in the combat control center might find news of our being in unusual danger of being rocketed of interest...

I'd no sooner gotten those words out of my mouth than the first of about a dozen rockets shrieked to the ground and exploded somewhere nearby, setting off sirens, cannon fire, etc. One of the card players, the watch supervisor, remarked, without looking up from his cards, "They know."

---

* They got a food delivery from the infamous chow hall about midnight every night. It wasn't great, but it was the only food available at midnight.

Back to the Navy medic thing, my favorite incident with them was one day when I'd made the mistake of eating in the chow hall, and got to feeling sicker and sicker to the point of almost passing out. I managed to get over to Sick Bay, which was this hot and muggy underground bunker, and staggered up to the intake desk, which was staffed by a corpsman in a crisp white uniform. With his pen poised over his logbook he asked me, "And what can we do for you?"

I opened my mouth to reply but instead of words coming out I barfed all over him, his desk, his logbook, everything. He didn't bat an eye. He just said, "Oh. Okay. Go sit over there," pointing to a bench across the room. He was so absolutely deadpan and I was so mortally embarrassed that I started to laugh and I guess I passed out. I woke up in a bed with all kinds of fluid tubes in me. The intake corpsman, in a clean uniform, stopped by to see how I was doing and joked that all the tubes weren't really necessary but rather were his revenge for my barfing on him. Nice guy.

Once the roads dried out somewhat from the monsoons and/or once they got Liberty Bridge built again (apparently the other side kept blowing it up), I did my courier runs to Da Nang driving a jeep in a 15-20 vehicle convoy with every third vehicle being a tank. We'd drive it at breakneck speed, frequently taking sniper fire. Sometimes someone in the convoy would return fire, but usually we'd just go faster. It was probably 25 years after I was home before I stopped scanning the tree line for muzzle flashes when driving out in the country.

Chapter Ten
Medcap, Marines, and Mud

Out in the villages on my Medcap runs, life was getting more and more interesting. It was easier to buy things - even bullets - out there than to try to get them through the regular supply system, and if you weren't a jerk you would start to make friends among the villagers.

One such friendship is of particular note: One day we were out in this village treating people when I noticed a little boy, probably five years old, peeking around from behind some other people, with big open fly-covered sores all over his skinny little legs. You knew he really needed to get those treated, and you sensed that he knew it too, but it would take a brave little kid to take the initiative on something like that.

I went a little ways off to the side, away from the noise and activity and squatted down as the Vietnamese do and just waited until he happened to glance my way. I smiled. He quickly looked away, but just a few seconds later he looked back. I smiled again. He smiled. I reached in my pocket and pulled out a pack of gum. He was definitely watching me now. I pointed at it, at him, and at the corpsmen. He understood, and after giving it some thought he came over and took my offered hand and we went up and got him cleaned up and bandaged, with him maintaining a death grip on my hand the whole time. It must have hurt, but he was a trooper. I handed one of the generally rude Vietnamese interpreters some money and told him that I wanted him to very gently tell my friend that he needed to keep those bandages on, and keep them clean and dry, and that we would be back in a few days to change them. We did come back, and sure enough there was my friend with clean and dry bandages still on. It cost me a pack of gum every time, but pretty soon we got him healed up okay.

Not long after that I was bored one day when things were pretty slow medically in that same hamlet, so I decided that I would go take a walk down by the river. I headed that way and had maybe gone 15 yards down the trail when something barreled into me like a small freight train from behind and wrapped itself around my legs, crying and pulling me back toward the village. It was the kid. I wasn't sure what was up, but there was no way he was letting me go any further on the trail, so we went back to the truck and I asked one of the interpreters to ask him what the trouble was with me walking down to the river? "Ambush," was the reply.

That was actually kind of a surprise, because as a general rule the VC and the Medcap team got along pretty well. We didn't exchange Christmas cards or anything like that, but they were cool about us going and being places they wouldn't have been cool about other Marines going or being. As previously mentioned, if they had a meeting going on or something that they didn't want us to interrupt, they'd fire some tracer rounds over the bow of our truck, and we'd fire a few rounds back (generally my fire-breathing Tommy gun) so we could all save face, and we'd just go on to the next village.

In the villages I cannot tell you how many times I'd be sitting around chewing the fat with some of the locals when something would be said about the Viet Cong, and they'd all start giggling. I would slap my forehead (which always highly amused them) and complain, "You guys aren't VC are you?", which would really set them off laughing, at which point I would form my hand into a simulated pistol – we were all sitting there armed to the teeth with real weapons by the way - and announce that in the name of the United States Marine Corps they were all under arrest, they would laugh, and we'd end up talking about stuff.

Literally every VC I ever talked about it with was a convert to that side as a result of some stupid thing some American GI or group of GIs had done to him, his family, or his village. Few of them appeared to have more than a very rudimentary understanding of communism, except that it meant getting rid of the landlords (generally absentee land barons who'd been given large land grants for their loyalty and service to France) and getting rid of us, which for most of them was quite enough. Very nice folks, all of them I ever talked with.

Only once did we have a potentially serious situation develop while we were out Medcapping: We'd set up shop in a hamlet and an hour or so into it a major fire-fight broke out in the next hamlet over, maybe 400 yards away. We hastily set up a perimeter, but the people in the hamlet we were in didn't seem too worried, and no one came charging across the rice paddies at us, so we let whoever it was over there carry on with whatever it was they were doing.

One particularly interesting thing which developed over time from those village visits was that I somehow became an informal liaison between the local VC command and my Regiment's CO. We'd just be chatting along out in the village and one of the people would let drop something very specific such as, "We hear that Charlie and Delta Companies, 2nd Battalion, are going to Hill 597 next Tuesday at 0700 hours; that is a very bad plan." I would dutifully nod and murmur something like, "Is that so...?" and they'd nod, and we'd go onto other things.

When we got back to An Hoa, I'd look up the Regimental CO (we had a new one then who everyone loved) and report that out in the villages they didn't think sending Charlie and Delta Companies of the 2nd Battalion up Hill 597 next Tuesday morning at 0700 hours was a good plan. And his mouth would drop open, and then clamp shut, followed generally by a few colorful phrases and a protest that "They can't know that! That is Top Secret information!"

The trouble was that everything we did had to be shared with the local ARVN forces, and the ARVN knew the war was lost, so almost everything Secret or Top Secret quickly got itself passed on to the other side as some ARVN officer or other tried to position himself to survive the change.

Generally my conveying one of those sorts of messages to the Regimental CO would result in the operation being canceled, which was, I think, why this informal passing of information had been started - to minimize casualties on both sides while the war ground to its inevitable ending. But several times when our CO groused that he was under pressure from Division to do "something"* I dutifully communicated that fact back out in the village, and as often as not I would be reassured in a conversation an hour or so later that "It probably would

*   His actual words were closer to "You tell those sonsabitches that the 5th Marines cannot just stay in their barracks!"

be okay" for such and such a mission to go ahead after all. Although a few people stepped on booby traps or tripped over tree roots, etc. no one ever got into a big fire fight on one of those missions where we'd had that little exchange of information and I had been given an okay for the mission to go ahead.

Meanwhile, guard duty remained its colorful self. One had to pity the poor officers (often the newest in-country, lowest-ranking people available) who were assigned the thankless task of giving us our orders for the night. We all knew when and where we were to assemble every day when we'd been assigned to guard duty, so we'd all be there with all our normal and extra weapons, ammo, etc. Then the poor Officer of the Guard would show up, at least the first time they had that duty probably expecting everyone to jump up and stand at attention. But no one did anything close to that. Everyone just pretty much stayed where they were (laying on the ground, hanging off the side of a bunker, etc.) and kept doing whatever they were doing (smoking, playing cards, reading, etc.).

Any effort the officer might put into changing that was doomed, since the brig was safer and drier than guard duty. So he'd have to just overlook everyone's "unmilitary" behavior and herd us off to the appropriate places as best he could. An incident that kind of stands out in all of that is one time when the officer person tried to get someone to carry a radio out on a listening post. The prospective radioman insisted he was not going to do it (I assume because radio operators are snipers' favorite target). They went back and forth about it and finally the officer thrust the radio into the guy's hands, insisting on his taking it. The guy tossed it on the ground, shot it full of holes, and told the officer that if he gave him another one, he'd kill it too!

We had a somewhat similar situation occur when some folks from some Defense Department contractor showed up all proud and happy about the new field radio they either were making or hoped to make to replace the big old heavy brick-like radios we were using. They arrived on a chopper all in brand new jungle utilities (uniforms) that obviously had been ironed, and proudly displayed the radio system they had developed, which was an array of different little components connected by little wires all mounted on a nylon web vest sort of thing.

The minute we saw it we had a vague suspicion how the old Gunnery Sergeant who ran our Platoon's Radio Section was going to react, so a crowd of us quickly gathered. Sure enough, Gunny came out of the Radio... place? Calling it an "office" would be a stretch. Anyway, he was a sweet old guy, we all seriously loved him, but he was "Old Corps" 100% and was so covered with hair that he was like a big old bear. He had been summoned to come see what he was to start sending his people (who he was immensely/intensely protective of) out into the field with so that this contractor could make a mint selling their crap to the government.

He just stood there chomping on his cigar glaring at the contractor guy and at the new radio while the guy rattled through all the wondrous things it had and was and could do. When the guy finished his pitch, Gunny reached over and took the vest/radio and scrutinized it for a second before whipping it over his head and smacking it on the ground as hard as he could, causing even those of us who had anticipated such a thing to jump a little. Gunny then picked up the radio and tried to turn it on; it was obviously broken in about a dozen places. (I should mention here that the radios we were using could be tossed around all day without failing.) He tossed it back to the contractor guy and said, "I won't send my troops into danger with this piece of shit." and stomped off back to his lair, leaving the contractor standing there with his mouth hanging open. That was the last we heard of it.

We were less fortunate on the teletype front. One day we received a shipment of "new and improved" teletype equipment that we were ordered to begin using; with said orders also directing us to destroy our old equipment. But one quick look at the new gear suggested that like the above radio, this new stuff was not made for the conditions we were operating in, and indeed that quickly proved to be the case. So thank goodness we ignored the order to destroy the old gear. Instead we hid it in our "crypto" room, and each time the new stuff failed, which it did quite regularly, we'd drag out and plug in the old machines that would chug away through anything.

What seemed to most offend the new gear was any sort of vibration or shaking of the ground. Unfortunately one of our neighbors was a battery of guns, which I was told were the largest land-based cannons the U.S. then possessed. They were huge, awesome. I don't know if it is true or not, but I was told they could throw a 200 lb. shell 25 miles. They certainly looked like they could!

They were so big they had to lower the barrels to parallel with the ground to load them. Then they would crank them up into a shooting position. Whenever you saw one of them cranking up, it was a very good idea to try to put a wall of some sort between you and it, and to hunker down and cover your ears as best you could, because when they fired, it was so loud it would shake the ground and rattle your teeth - and totally screw up our new fancy-dancy teletype equipment.

God help anyone sent out into the field with only that new equipment. Maybe it was faster or somehow "better" than what it replaced, but what it replaced was indestructible, and the new stuff would go down every time the gun battery fired, which was normally several times a day.

This is a digression, but I suppose I should mention, if only to honor those who died in the incident, that one time one of the big guns exploded when they fired it. I was clear over on the other side of the base when it happened, but it was clear the instant it did that that was the wrong kind of "boom", and then big chunks of metal started falling all over the place out of the sky. I never did hear how many people died, but I assume it took out the entire gun crew.

But back to guard duty, one quickly learned that at An Hoa during the monsoon season it was advisable to walk behind a tall person on the way out to the perimeter. One time I was following a tall guy carrying an M-60 machine gun on his shoulder who stepped in a deep spot in the mud and simply disappeared without a trace! A second later a hand appeared, we grabbed it/him, and got him out, but no one volunteered to go down there and try to find the M-60.

Then there was this guy who was reassigned to our Regiment from someplace else, likely to save his life, who immediately proved himself to be a menace to society. I had to ban him from the MedCap team after I caught him going door to door in a village offering women money for sex. Nobody liked to be around him because (1) he was generally obnoxious* and (2) the man was a freaking arsenal just waiting to explode! I have never seen a person voluntarily carry that much firepower: multiple rifles, half ton of ammo, knives, a dozen or more hand grenades with their pins straightened (the pins are bent so they can't accidentally fall out, but that makes them hard to pull, so this rocket scientist decided to straighten all of them...), and that was for just being on base! In the field he was like Rambo on drugs!

In any case, one night when I was on guard duty out on the perimeter, I was sitting up on the roof of our guard bunker writing letters by moonlight to Congresspeople about their needing to stop this stupid war, when all of a sudden all holy hell broke loose. Bullets were punching into sandbags all around me and zipping around my head. I fell flat, rolled off the roof, and was back in the bunker firing up our M-60 machine gun when a call came in over the radio that we should hold fire because that was just our buddy "Ace" out on a Listening Post taking pot shots at a dog he'd seen.

Three different bunkers pleaded to be allowed to kill him. Permission was denied. But it was the prerogative of people on guard duty to fire pop-flares over the barbed wire out in front of them whenever they suspected there might be enemy movement out there, so for the rest of the night all three bunkers took turns shooting pop flares over the Listening Post in hopes that the Viet Cong or

---

* Among other things, although his name was something like 'Clarance' he insisted that everyone call him 'Ace', and after a few weeks it was discovered he'd doctored his Service Record Book to give himself several promotions and medals he hadn't earned, but he was quick to make sure everyone knew he was 'a born-again Christian', etc.

NVA or God Almighty or someone would take advantage of their being all lit up and kill them. No dice. Damn! We eventually transferred him on to some other unit where he eventually reportedly did get hurt (but not killed) in a "friendly fire" incident of some sort...

A much more serious incident occurred that spring that still gives me twinges to think about: A flight (a couple of choppers) of Recon troops had stopped by An Hoa for some reason on their way out on a mission and the two choppers had accidentally gotten too close together and had locked blades, which caused both of them to flip, explode and burn with everyone still on board. They had just landed, so they were on the ground when the accident occurred, but a lot of people still got hurt. I was on the LZ at the time and was involved in the rescue part.

Be darned if they didn't decide to go ahead with the mission using everyone who wasn't so badly hurt they couldn't go. So they flew out an hour or two later (in different choppers obviously), and apparently flew into or later got into a major ambush and needed to be rescued out. The CO of the Recon Battalion (the place I stayed in Da Nang) himself led the rescue effort, and with him and them hanging from netting under a chopper, it and they flew into the side of a mountain and were all killed. They weren't even our guys, and God only knows we were losing enough of our own, but I think that loss hurt us all more than any other we suffered during the year I was there. There was a lot of respect between the 5th Marines and 1st Recon.

I mentioned earlier that personal hygiene was a pretty elusive commodity during the monsoon season because we were wet and muddy all the time. My nose is bad enough that I don't recall it being a problem for me when I arrived, but it was kind of fun when new people would arrive ever after. They would walk into a tent or someplace for the first time and just turn green from the smell of us. It wasn't like we'd become complete animals or anything - we did wash when we could - but just with the mud and the blood and the crud you were in all the time it wasn't likely that even the best efforts could bring you up to even a respectable junkyard level.

I never really thought about exactly how far down the scale we were until years later when I was reflecting on an incident and decided that maybe it did indicate that a certain level of degeneration or derangement had been achieved: One night during the monsoons I was out on guard duty and was taking my turn to sleep. There wasn't anywhere to sleep but in the mud, but we had rigged up a little shelter so at least your head and top part of your body wouldn't be directly in the rain. So I was sleeping away, and woke up to find that a rat had swum over, climbed up onto my chest, and was sitting there grooming himself! I kicked him off, rolled over, and went back to sleep, muttering about how he could go find a dry spot of his own...

Chapter Eleven
Politics

The war was getting uglier and uglier. The peace movement and Richard Nixon were trying to outdo one another, with the peace folks holding bigger and bigger peace demonstrations, and Nixon doing more and more bombing and other things to try to convince the NVA/VC (and the peace movement) to give up. Among the 50-100 Marines I had day-to-day contact with, only one or two had any use whatsoever for Nixon or the war. It was a crock of you-know-what simply to be endured.

Once, the Los Angeles Free Press decided to do a collage or article or something on the theme of things that are green, and asked people to send in interesting green things. I chanced across a very pretty little flower blooming out of a hole in a green sandbag in a blast wall on base and took a picture of it and submitted it with a little note about much I was looking forward to peace replacing war. I showed it to a couple people and they wanted to sign it too, and word got out, and before I could get it mailed off I had over a hundred unsolicited signatures from other Marines on it.

One thing that did rattle me a little bit was a similar incident: I had chatted with a number of people about the anti-war press movement, and had showed them several of the papers that got forwarded to me in Vietnam. Be darned if one of them (communicators were the only people with access to printing equipment) didn't start a paper at An

Hoa! That was the last thing I needed to get blamed for. Fortunately (for me) it only lasted an issue or two, and never came up in my case.

I should mention for the historic record two things of note relating to the larger war effort:

The first thing was Nixon's much-heralded "bringing of troops home" effort, which at least in its early stages was one of the crueler jokes of history. What they did when they picked a unit to return to the U.S. was transfer out of it everyone who still had more than a few months to serve in Vietnam, and transfer in a bunch of short-timers from other units, so what actually returned to the U.S. was the unit's flag and a bunch of people who were due to go home anyway. In the meantime it filled units like ours to overflowing with more people than we knew what to do with. I actually had a day off once or twice we had so many people! (Until then we worked at least 12 hours on, 12 off, 7 days a week.)

The other was the discovery up by Hue City of mass graves of hundreds of civilians. The Nixon Administration quickly branded it as evidence of how evil the other side was, and said that when the bad guys had taken over Hue during the Tet Offensive in 1968 they had come in with lists of people to execute and had summarily performed those executions and buried all those people to hide the evidence. Forty plus years later that remains the most widely accepted explanation of what happened at Hue and how those mass graves came into being.

But the 5th Marines had been one of the lead units in the fight to retake the city, and we still had some people who had extended their tours in Vietnam who had been there. They just rolled their eyes at Nixon's bullshitting the entire world and getting away with it. I first talked with a couple of people about it just by accident, but then began systematically seeking people out to ask, and from them all I heard exactly the same story: The bad guys had no time, no opportunity, no equipment, and no access to the places where the graves were. From the moment they took the city they were fighting for their lives, having been surrounded and cut off by our forces. In the days that followed there occurred some of the most brutal house-to-house fighting in history, with nary a reference ever in the news to how many civilian casualties that might result in. The city is retaken, the U.S. rejoices, and when later these big graves are discovered, Nixon parades out his lie, and the world buys it!

What the people who'd been there told me was that in that fight you couldn't afford to worry about hurting innocent bystanders - before you went into a room you tossed a grenade in, or sprayed it with machine gun fire. If something moved, you shot it. And you certainly didn't have any time or stomach for taking prisoners. There were no prisoners, only lots of dead folks, some shot in the head from up close. Bad p.r. So the dump trucks came in and the front-end-loaders and bodies got scooped up and dumped and covered over, and all we've got is a bunch of people unaccounted for... They must have gone off to stay with relatives in the country, don't you think?

The size and placement of the graves makes it virtually impossible for the other side to have been responsible for creating them. They had no time or equipment for digging anything that size or for carrying that many bodies, and if they did, why exactly would they go through our lines to do it? It makes no sense, but to this day the evil communist murder of innocent civilians in Hue City remains the explanation of that whole incident that most of the world believes.

On April 30, 1970, U.S. and South Vietnamese forces invaded Cambodia. The next 30 days were the weirdest and certainly among the most difficult of my life. When word of the invasion spread in America, protests quickly escalated to civil disorder to a level resulting in the call-up of National Guard troops in a majority of states. Hundreds of colleges and universities shut down altogether. Millions of people were in the streets protesting. And, frankly, it wasn't much different in Vietnam.

I was absolutely appalled by the expansion of the war to this whole new arena, and so was everyone around me. It just freaked me out, it was the proverbial last straw. So I walked over to the Company office (Headquarters Company, which the Communications Platoon was part of) and laid my M-16 on the duty NCO's desk and told him that I quit. He sputtered that you can't just quit, but I assured him that I indeed had just done precisely that. He said I should go talk to the Chaplain to see if he could get my head straightened out or whatever it needed.

I wandered over there, but the Chaplain was out earning combat pay flying a Huey gunship (which has no function except killing people), so his assistant helpfully suggested that I go talk to the Regimental Legal Officer instead since I was certain to be court martialed. I found the guy packing books in boxes. He looked up and asked what he could do for me? I told him I had just quit the Marine Corps and that I had been told to come see him about getting court martialed. He whooped with laughter and shook my hand and said that he'd love to help me, but that HE had just quit too! As an officer he could do that, of course. It wasn't just we peons who saw the invasion of Cambodia as the last straw.

Thus began a strange period of limbo where I wasn't really working for the Marine Corps anymore, but since I couldn't really leave or stop wearing their uniform (since I had nowhere to go and nothing else to wear), I found myself kind of hanging around trying to draw someone's attention to the fact that I had indeed quit. A few days later I was promoted to Corporal.

In the meantime, the entire U.S. had just gone up for grabs. The news was full of huge protests against the invasion of Cambodia. Then on May 4 there was the shooting of protesters at Kent State University. Something like 90% of the colleges and universities in the U.S. closed down. It sounded like America had finally decided enough was enough.

I did keep doing the MedCap runs, since those felt more like I was working for the Vietnamese people than for our government. When I got back to the base from one of those somebody told me that word had come over that I was to report to the Regimental Intelligence Officer. Not a good sign, since he wasn't someone I regularly visited. So I walked over there and on his desk was this document, about an inch and a half thick, with the logo of the Naval Investigative Service and my name in big letters. Not good.

He picked it up and snarled at me that he'd received this report on my various misdeeds as an anti-war organizer back in the States, and at the very least they were going to terminate my security clearance and who knows what else? As he was saying that he was flipping it at me - the only time I ever got to see it - and I noted that it was just full of pictures of me at various rallies and with people I never took any pictures of, and even had copies of lots of my handwriting and of our newspaper from North Carolina.

He repeated that they were going to jerk my clearance, and said that I could write a statement in defense of myself if I wanted to. I asked him if I could read the report so that I knew what I was accused of being or doing? How silly of me! We're talking military justice here, not real justice, so of course they never let me read it.

So I went off and the first thing I did was write a letter to my Individuals Against the Crime of Silence friends telling them that the proverbial shit had finally hit the fan, that my situation was very precarious, and that I didn't know what to expect in the days ahead. Then I spent a day or so writing a thing saying that I opposed the war and had worked to stop it and regarded both of those as patriotic acts, but that at no time in any of those activities had I abused whatever "secrets" had passed through my hands in my official capacity. I handed that in, and that was that. There wasn't any hearing or anything; no one ever really talked with me about it again. They jerked my clearance anyway.

So now there I was, without a job (since I had quit), and without the wherewithal to do that job even if I wanted to, since I no longer had a security clearance. So I bummed around for a few days, not really knowing what to expect, but somewhat afraid that I could possibly have an "accident" if the powers that be decided to go that route, and making some arrangements for how I might respond if that indeed appeared to be in the offing. But then I got a letter (or telegram?) from Ken Cloke, the head of the

Military Law Panel of the National Lawyers Guild, telling me that the Individuals Against the Crime of Silence people had been in touch with him, concerned about the very real possibility of something bad happening to me, and that they had given him all the background info, and that he was in touch with a UPI reporter who was already in Vietnam, and that I was to write him a letter every day for the rest of the time I was in Vietnam telling him that I was okay, and that if he ever went two days without getting such a letter, he and his UPI friend would be on their way to An Hoa to investigate in a heartbeat. The letter/telegram had been opened before I had gotten it, so the bad guys now also knew that I had friends.

A day or two later, the Communications Officer (the Major responsible for me being called Gunga Din) sauntered up and said he had a deal for me: Why didn't I come work for him full-time in the Communications Office just typing and doing filing and that sort of thing, with still an occasional courier run into Da Nang and all the MedCap runs I wanted, but no guns, no fuss, etc.? As contrasted with getting sent out on a night patrol and being brought back in a body bag, that sounded pretty reasonable, so I agreed, but within the week he got unexpected transfer orders back to the States (apparently he was suspected of some black market money doings). At almost the same moment our Regimental Commander (the one everyone hated, and who jerked my clearance) also rotated out.

As it turns out, the two of them (the Communications Officer and the Regimental Commander) were replaced by two of the most wonderful people I have ever known: Major David K. Shroyer as Communications Officer and Colonel C. V. Judge as Regimental CO. What a pair those two were! Both were Annapolis graduates and were straight arrows, but we got along famously from literally our first meeting. God only knows why! Can you imagine being the new commanding officer of a unit in a war zone and finding out that your assistant is this crazed anti-war activist?

What may have helped was my leveling with him (Major Shroyer) his first day there; I asked to talk with him and told him that he had a right to know who and what I was so that if he didn't want to keep me working in the office with him he could make that change. He said he thought he could handle the challenge, and we were friends ever after, to the point that in the fall he initiated and Col. Judge readily signed and forwarded on to Headquarters Marine Corps a request that my security clearance be restored. And they were the ones who put me up for my Navy Achievement Medal and gave me a Regimental Commendation when I left.

But their effort to get my security clearance restored ran into an unexpected complication: In the midst of all of the transfers and changes, my Naval Investigative Service file had been lost! The Intelligence Officer, old Regimental Commander, old Communications Officer, new Regimental Commander, and new Communications Officer all had it in their hands at one time or another, but then it disappeared off the face of the earth. It was really too bad, both because I would have liked to have had a copy, and because without it, it was impossible to get my clearance back.

When I finally did a "Freedom of Information Act" request for a copy of my file many years later, all they had was about 30 pages of material, including an angry exchange of letters between N.I.S. and the 5th Marines about where the file was. I never did find out what happened to it. Was it really accidentally lost, or did someone destroy it? I'll never know...

By mid June my life was on a somewhat even keel again, but I was sinking into what would probably be diagnosed as clinical depression. There had just been too many deaths, too many outrages. About then it was announced that since the area our Regiment had been dealing with had been "secured", we were going to turn it over to the South Vietnamese Army and go somewhere else.

What a bunch of horse manure that was! Secured? In somebody's dreams maybe! If anything it was more dangerous than ever. But Mr. Nixon's lies to the American people had to have us "winning", so our area was declared "won", and the 51st ARVN (51st South Vietnamese Army Regiment) was flown in on C-130s so that they could make a symbolic sweep through an area nearby which we affectionately called "the Arizona Territory" before taking official possession of An Hoa and the whole area around it. Apparently nobody told the other side about the "symbolic" nature of the ARVN's sweep, because they got the holy hell kicked out of them, and the survivors came scrambling back across the river as fast as they could run.

I was one of the last 500 or so Marines to leave An Hoa. That was weird, particularly on the heels of what had just happened not that far away to our replacements. I think that was about the only time in Vietnam when I really had the jitters about getting killed in a big shoot-out with the other side. It would have been a public relations coup to kick our butts out of there, but all that happened was a minor flesh wound: As we were pulling out they discovered all this junk that people had been ignoring for a long time, and one of the things was this fairly large quantity (maybe 10,000 reams) of moldy paper for Top Secret messages that had been in a musty, damp back corner of some underground bunker since forever.

It is probably supposed to be a secret that each kind of classified message gets printed on a distinctively different kind of paper that is used for nothing else, but oh well, now you know! (Don't tell anybody!) The most distinctive of these is Top Secret paper. Top Secret paper is sort of like the flag; you can't just toss it in the trash. There is a whole very elaborate ritual that has to be employed in destroying it. Step one is burning it, so I and a couple other people started carrying the paper out to be burned. I was walking along carrying a case when this ant showed up from someplace - off the case maybe - and wandered down to my hand. I didn't think anything of it until he reared back and took a bite and I felt like I had just been shot in the hand. It was a fire ant, the meanest motherfucking ant on the face of the earth, and it turned out that our precious paper was full of them.

My hand had swelled up like a balloon, so I went off to sick bay, leaving my friends to deal with the situation, the resolution of which I understand eventually came to involve incendiary grenades and high explosives.

Chapter Twelve
Hill 37 & LZ Baldy

We came to earth again on Hill 37, a modest little lump of a hill (the "37" in its name referred to how many feet high it was), which was about 25 miles closer to Da Nang than An Hoa. As the American people were being told that we were "winning" the war, we were actually just pulling back closer and closer to the coastal cities.

The interesting thing about being on Hill 37 was that it had been a French fort during their attempts to subdue the Vietnamese people. The old fortifications were still there, like ghosts of another era. The story that circulated was that the French officers had found Vietnamese women very attractive and that before anyone knew it they all had Vietnamese mistresses living with them, until one night at a prearranged time the mistresses all cut their officer's throats and opened the gate and let in Viet Minh forces to wipe out the garrison. I don't know if it was true or not, but it was a little unsettling to hear that within days of our leaving An Hoa the garrison (of South Vietnamese forces) left there had suffered a similar fate.

On Hill 37 we only had the Regimental HQ and maybe one or two Companies of regular infantry, which was a lot fewer people than we had had at An Hoa. Hill 37 also didn't have anywhere near the perimeter defenses An Hoa did, just a few coils of barbed wire piled on top of each other. I felt rather exposed, particularly one night when I was in the shower and all hell broke loose: There were explosions and small arms fire and sirens all over the place.

This was definitely not a drill, so the half dozen of us who were in the shower took off sprinting across the hilltop dressed as we'd come into the world, to a ditch we could dive in and ride out whatever was happening, which actually did turn out to be a fairly serious effort to overrun the base. It didn't last long, which was a good thing because the word had gotten out among the area's mosquitoes that there was an "all you can eat" buffet in the ditch, and we were all in danger of expiring from blood loss.

The most striking memory I have of Hill 37 is watching the launching of what was supposed to be a big operation probably 5 miles to the northwest of us. It began with B-52's doing this incredible bombing run, just pulverizing the area with what I assume were 500 and 1,000 lb. bombs which shook the ground even as far away as we were. Then choppers - the big double-rotary heavy horses - brought in big nets filled with barrels of napalm, which they released and then fired into to burn the area to a crisp. Finally Huey gunships flew over firing their machine guns, which supposedly can put a round in every square inch of an area the size of a football field in a matter of seconds.

When the first wave of three troop transport choppers went in to put troops on the ground, we could see the tracers arching up at them as they came in. One chopper bought it still in the air. Another was blown up on the ground. Only the third one made it back out again. And we were sitting there watching it like it was on TV or something. You know, just a bunch of people getting killed. The usual. Is there anything on any of the other channels? It was all very surreal.

Another interesting event was the day the Regimental Commander loaded up all of his Field Grade (Major and above) officers and they went off to visit a couple of places to our west where they were thinking about doing some operations (later discouraged by my in-village MedCap talks with the locals). They were all gone, so it was just us chickens back at the coop when in came a call that the Divisional Commander was on his way over for a surprise visit! Oh shit! So we called the Regimental Commander to tell him, and I started running around trying to find an officer willing to go down to the LZ and greet the Divisional Commander. Talk about wimps. None of them were willing.

So oh great, the Divisional CO is going to come out here for his first visit ever and no-fricking-body is going to be there to greet him? There was no way that could turn out well, so I decided to steal a jeep and go down to the LZ and pretend that I had been sent to give the Divisional Commander the Colonel's greetings and to transport him and his party up to where they could have some refreshments while awaiting the Colonel's imminent return from his inspection tour with his senior staff. It sounded just plausible enough to maybe work. At least someone would be there to salute when he stepped off the chopper, which would probably go over better than everyone hiding from him. So I drove down there and arrived as the Divisional CO's chopper and its two escorts swept in, kicking up the Mother of all Dust Storms, in the midst of which the Regimental Commander's chopper came tearing in from the west and landed as well. I saw the two of them salute and shake hands, and I quietly turned my jeep around and scooted away.

I believe that we were only on Hill 37 for a few weeks before word came down that we were going to move again as part of a simultaneous shift of three Regiments more or less from the north to the south: The 1st Marines (known as "The Palace Guard", since they usually guarded Da Nang) were sweeping south and would take over Hill 37 and much of what the 5th Marines had been covering, the 5th would sweep south and take over what the 7th Marines had been covering, and the 7th would load on ships and go home. It sounded easy enough, but in the 11th hour of the planning process the Logistics shack on Hill 37 got rocketed and both the plans and the planners for getting us safely off the Hill and into our new place were summarily lost.

By then a lot of officers were using the Comm Office as a hang-out, bumming coffee, reading my L.A. Free Presses, East Village Others, etc. - and it quickly became clear to me that they hadn't a clue how to get us moved. So I took a clipboard and some paper and made the rounds talking with the NCOs on the Hill, and from those conversations I drew up a plan, which I presented to the Regimental CO. He studied it, and then asked me, "Will this work?"

I smiled and said that it had better, because I had put him and me on the last chopper leaving. He whooped with laughter, studied it some more, and it ended up being the plan we used. (And I am pleased to report that it went off without a hitch.)

The only skullduggery of the move was that the Commander of the 7th Marines had somehow come into possession of a very cute little puppy, which Colonel Judge had taken a real shine to. Apparently there was little love lost between the two Regimental Commanders, and the next thing I knew I was being furtively handed said puppy by Colonel Judge and ordered to "hide it!" I decided the puppy was probably a cryptography specialist and should camp out in the Top Secret crypto part of the Comm Center until the 7th Marine-folk went away. It almost touched off a war between the two Regiments, but they had ships to get on and couldn't take the time to disassemble Hill 37 looking for it, so we ended up with a mascot, and I ended up with "puppy care" added to my list of duties.

Our new home had been called LZ Baldy, but got renamed Marine Corps Combat Base Baldy in honor of its new residents. It was bigger than Hill 37, but smaller than An Hoa, and was down by Hoi An and Tam Ky, south of Da Nang. It was much more like Divisional Headquarters than either An Hoa or Hill 37 had been. It didn't have sidewalks or mowed lawns, but was much more proper, to the point of people wearing rank insignia, saluting, and even shining their boots. What a drag. It was like being back in the Marine Corps again.

Despite our step up in the world, we remained rather under-equipped in a lot of ways. For example, we didn't have chairs, or at least not enough of them. And we still had never been issued dishes or silverware for the chow hall. Stuff like that. When Col. Judge heard that all of the 7th Marines' equipment was to be turned over to the South Vietnamese Army he went ballistic, and the next thing you know there was a five truck convoy on its way from Baldy to Chu Lai where all that stuff was being warehoused, with oral orders to "requisition" whatever we could get our hands on. His specific request to me was chairs for his officers to sit in during their briefings. We saluted our way though the gates, found the warehouses, coaxed them open with bolt-cutters, and loaded up tons of materials, including several dozen plush V.I.P. chairs that I and my cab-mounted M-50 machine gun guarded all the way back to Baldy.

I guess I can't complain about life on Baldy, except that it was way too spit and polish for my tastes. It really wasn't spit and polish at all, but next to An Hoa it sure felt that way.

The officers put up a volleyball net next to the Comm Office, which once again had become their hang-out. As a result, I ended up like MASH's Radar O'Reilly, running around and doing their work for them, including handling all kinds of classified materials they didn't seem to care about my handling. When a radio message would come in that required a decision of some sort to be made, the Comm Center people would always give it to me (for some reason they were afraid of the officers), and I would have to go out and try to get the appropriate person's attention as they continued to play their fast and furious games of volleyball.

I would whistle and wave my arms and call out the officer's name, and while keeping his eyes on the ball he'd generally say, "Yah, yah, Gunga, what'da ya got?" If it was a classified message I would say, "It's a secret!", and they would all start laughing and giving me a ration of shit about keeping secrets. I would sternly remind them that there were rules about such things, and that there was, in fact, a war going on, and that the secret I had pertained to that very war. Often they would just tell me to go ahead and take care of the matter. If I did, I would loop back later to double-check with the officer to make sure what

I'd decided and done was okay. But if it was too important for that, I would persist until he gave up and came over to make the needed decision.

The only Field Grade officer who didn't get into all of that was the Regiment's Executive Officer, who I think hated the CO and I know hated me. If anything ever happened to the CO, that character would have toasted me in a heartbeat.

By this time it was getting toward monsoon season again, and the first big named operation (Tulare Falls?) our Regiment did that fall, along with some U.S. Army folks and some ARVN forces got itself washed out when a typhoon decided to complicate the already soggy monsoon conditions by attaching itself to the coast just east of us. All the low-lying ground in that part of Vietnam flooded, and Tulare Falls became a search and rescue operation, bringing our troops back along with thousands of civilians (or more properly, thousands of Vietnamese people who were all supposed to all be civilians), with choppers landing left and right all over the place day and night dropping off bunches of cold, wet, hungry, frightened people and zooming away to go find more. I think I worked around the clock for four or five days straight going out and greeting groups of people and trying to reassure them that they would be well-treated, and then trying to make sure that that happened.

Some of my peers did not relate so warmly or comfortably to the Vietnamese as I did, but most people knew I had the CO's ear and so gave me whatever I asked for. The number of people needing help was off the charts, far more than we could properly accommodate, but at least with us they were on high ground above the flooding. We were later awarded a Vietnamese Cross of Gallantry for our efforts. It sounds like a more impressive award than it really is, but it felt good about being part of a rescue/relief effort instead of being part of getting people killed.

After the typhoon went away and the water receded enough so that everyone could go back home again and military operations could resume, be darned if they didn't decide to start up the same silly big operation again, now called Operation Tulare Falls II. Bunches of people were going to be tromping all over hell's half acre looking for trouble. I didn't have to go, but one day when I carried some trash from our office down to where you dumped things for the garbage haulers (Vietnamese contractors) to take away, I noticed that peeking out of that big stinking pile of trash was something that shouldn't be there: some of the kind of paper that only Top Secret messages are supposed to be printed on.

I jumped the fence and pulled it out and Holy Shit, it was a full probably 50-page copy of the Operations Order for Tulare Falls II. I didn't read it, of course, but I knew that such documents typically include every detail worth knowing about who is going where with what kind of support to try to achieve what objectives while using what radio frequencies and call signs, etc., etc. Just about everything anyone would need to know in order to spring a perfect ambush.

I quickly looked through the immediately surrounding garbage to see if it had any companions, scanned the whole pile for the same, and then vaulted back over the fence, grabbed a couple of other Marines and ordered them to stand guard and not let anybody in there until I or someone else came and okayed that. I sprinted up to the Regimental CO's office, walked in (under the circumstances I truly did forget to knock and all those other rituals), and laid the Operations Order face down on his desk in front of him, announcing, "Sir, I just found this down in the garbage pit, and if it was there, there might be others..."

He turned it over, realized what it was, and the color drained from his face. Blowing past the XO, who was hoping to chastise me for failing to observe proper protocols, the chain of command, and blah, blah, blah (the man had a serious Type A personality...), we stopped by the Comm Office where he put the Comm Officer to work tracking down where the Operations Order had come from (each copy is numbered, and they keep track of who got which number), and gathered up some other "Communicators" (because they had security clearances and knew the types of paper classified messages are printed on) and we went dumpster-diving for the rest of the afternoon.

In the end we didn't find anything else. It was just that one copy that some Army officer had read, copied down the stuff that pertained to him, and then pitched, apparently without giving a thought to the possible consequences of its falling into the wrong hands.

As my time in Vietnam was winding down, I was surprised one day to receive in the mail not just one, but two official copies of the War Resisters League's Annual Peace Award for 1970. The League had, since its creation in 1923 following World War I, opposed participation in wars in every way, shape and form, and had generally focused on people who had gone to prison rather than serve. But in the craziness of Vietnam they realized that there were some of us who were doing what needed to be done from within the military itself, and decided to honor that. And it was indeed an honor.

Since before I had arrived in Vietnam, the deal had been that if you had less than a year left on your enlistment when your tour over there ended, they would just let you go when you returned to the states. They wanted to keep a few people to help train new folks, but they certainly didn't want or need the entire crazy mass of us. I would only have 10 months left on my enlistment, so all I needed to do was survive a few more weeks and I would be free and clear. Or so I thought until one night when I was over at the Comm Center (I still had no clearance to be there; but it was late at night, I was hungry, and that was where the food was!). I was reading the messages that, as usual, were piling up while the traditional card game preempted any of the real watch standers from paying attention to anything, when I came across an order canceling the "early out" program.

My howl of pain sent the room into pandemonium, and once they learned the source of my anguish they joined their voices to mine in cursing anything and everything that came to mind with every expletive we could remember or invent for the occasion. NOOOOOOOOOOOOOOOOOOOOOO! Not 10 more months, not back in the States with inspections, and haircuts, and all of that crap, not to mention in my case the little detail of being a known anti-war activist.

That was the worst part of it: They hadn't canceled the early-out program across the board, but only for certain occupational specialties, including mine, but since I no longer had a security clearance I couldn't do the job anyway! It was the worst of all worlds, and there was just no way in hell that I was going to be able to pull off 10 months of stateside spit-and-polish duty with all of that hanging over my head. I thought I was dead.

A few weeks later my orders arrived. I was to be assigned to the 9th Communications Battalion (a radio training school) at 29 Palms, California, a place that even in the Marine Corps is regarded as being just up the street a bit from Hell itself. My buddies (Col. Judge and Major Shroyer) on Baldy tried to help as best they could. They sent off letters trying to get my security clearance restored. They even toyed with the idea of trying to change my Occupational Specialty to one that did still qualify for early-outs, but none of the ones that they logically could switch me to did.

In the end they put me up for a Navy Achievement Medal, gave me some amazing 4.9 "Conduct and Proficiency" scores,* and awarded me a Regimental Commendation (called a "Meritorious Mast" in the Marine Corps) on my final day. I think I mentioned back when I noted how I came to be called "Gunga Din" ("Gunga" for short), that when Col. Judge stepped in front of me in this fairly formal ceremony attended by most of the Regimental Headquarters' Field Grade officers how he read along "...pleased to present to Corporal John M. Arnold..." ...and then he stopped, looked puzzled, looked up at me and asked, "Is that your name, Gunga?" which just set the whole group rolling on the floor. I admonished, "Sir,

---

* Every six months, or whenever you get promoted or transferred, your unit gave you a numeric rating of how you had behaved yourself and done your job. The ratings were on a scale of 0 to 5.0, and it was a little like the Richter scale in that the higher you got the more distance there was between those tenths of a point. A 4.9 more or less implied that you could literally walk on water!

this is an official ceremony. You are supposed to behave yourself!" ...which set them off again. It was pretty wild.

I hated that war more than I can ever express, but when those guys and I all shook hands for the last time mine weren't the only eyes with tears in them. What a blessing that I fell in with such a wonderful bunch of people...

Chapter Thirteen
Home Sweet Home?

The trip to Da Nang was probably the second worst fearing-for-one's-life experience of my time in Vietnam. They had monkeyed around and monkeyed around getting stuff ready for the three of us who were leaving that day. The problem was that they didn't have a good typist available, and with the old manual typewriters we were using, the typist had to be good or documents came out looking like hell. It was late in the day, and when I learned what was what was holding us up, I jumped in and quickly typed everything myself!

But it was too late, we had already missed the last chopper of the day, so they had to load us into a jeep at dusk and send us to drive unarmed - you have to turn in your weapons before you leave your unit - and in the dark and rain the 30-50 miles, whatever it was, up to Da Nang. We were all as certain as we could be that death was waiting around every corner. An ambush. A remote-controlled mine. Heck, some kid with spitballs! But we made it without incident.

The next morning we got processed and then they herded us out toward an airplane that was unloading new troops just arriving in country. It was a mirror image of what I had experienced a year earlier. The arriving soldiers looked so young and clean and innocent, I could barely stand to look at them. God only knows how we looked to them. Like the dregs of hell I suspect.

I should mention that prior to our walking out onto the tarmac, we each were given a moment by ourselves with our sea bag in these little out-house-like structures that had posters in them listing all the things that we could not take with us, and indicating that we would have several minutes to quietly discard any such things we might still possess. Once we stepped out of the little out-house thing, we were subject to being searched, and if we were found to still be in possession of any of the banned things, we would be going to the brig instead of home.

It was an amazing list of prohibited possessions, but what was even more amazing was gazing down the hole where people were to discard the banned things and seeing what all was there: Weapons, ammunition, explosives, drugs aplenty, and then all sorts of human body parts (one assumes Vietnamese body parts), all nicely dried or otherwise preserved as "souvenirs": fingers, ears, penises, breasts, noses, and God only knows what else. One assumes that they cleaned those places out fairly often, so everything I saw in just one of the maybe six or eight out-house things they had may well have come from just the guys on my flight alone.

The flight was a regular Pan Am commercial jet, complete with all the stuff they had on their regular civilian flights, including perky little stewardesses in short dresses who asked us if we wanted anything? And I think that is when it all really crashed in on me. I couldn't answer. I couldn't even look at them. I put my head down and closed my eyes and didn't open them again until we landed and I could get away from those people who were from such a totally different world than I was.

They took us to Okinawa where they unloaded

us and, after checking us in to a processing center, gave us shore liberty, the first most of us had had in a year. Another guy from my unit and I went into town, and for the first time in my life I got thoroughly drunk. He and I bribed the taxi driver who took us back to base, and the front gate guards to let the taxi take us all the way to our barracks to save us the pain, etc. of crawling from the gate to there on our bellies. The next morning they lined us up and read off the names of people who were flying out that day; I wasn't on the list.

Those of us who weren't flying out expected to get liberty again, but instead they said that we first had to go to a meeting of some sort. So we all dutifully went into this building and sat down in nice neat rows and it turned out to be a recruitment session for the VFW (Veterans of Foreign Wars). This guy told us how brave and wonderful we were and what a great job we'd done and wouldn't it be wonderful to be able to hang out with other veterans and stand united for the war and against those commie pink-o long-haired hippies who spit on the flag and blah, blah, blah... And who wants to be the first to sign up?

Not a single hand flinched. 200 Marines one day out of Vietnam sat perfectly still, and not a single one of us indicated any interest whatsoever in the B.S. this moron was trying to sell. He gave it a couple more tries, gave up, and they more or less released us. But they still hadn't given us shore leave, so we couldn't go anywhere - everybody was just milling around. Then they ordered us back into the meeting room again. We went in, but now there was some fairly distinct murmuring going on. The same guy got up, this time backed by some very piggy senior NCO, and they both harangued us about patriotism and the flag and bad old hippies, etc., and got basically the same response as at the first session, but this time with an edge of anger to it.

We spilled out and milled about some more, but still nothing was said about shore leave. And then, do you believe it, they ordered us back into the meeting room so the VFW recruiter could have a third go at us!?! This time when he stepped onto the stage, the first thing he had to do was dodge a chair, the first of many that were tossed onto the stage, through the windows, against the walls and lights, etc. as 200 now very angry Marines thoroughly dismantled that meeting room beyond the point where it could ever be used to torment folk like us again. We smashed and kicked and tore with the abandon of fiends released from captivity, and when we were done, we went on shore liberty, all 200 of us as a group, and no one ever said a word about the meeting room or about us leaving the base without orders.

The next day they did call my name, meaning I was scheduled to fly out that day, but when they finished reading the list they asked if anyone would be willing to give up their seat so that someone who was trying to get home for an emergency situation could do so. That sounded good to me, so I raised my hand and went to town and got drunk again. The next day the same thing happened: They called my name; they asked for volunteers to give up seats, I raised my hand, and went into town and got drunk.*

This began to dawn on me as possibly being a good career move: If people would just keep having emergencies, and I could keep raising my hand for only

---

*   That week in Okinawa was the only period of drunkenness of my entire life, but that week I truly drank myself into oblivion at every opportunity.

another 300 days, the Marine Corps and I might part as friends after all! My liver would be destroyed, but that was a small price to pay. But alas, they only let you do that so many times, and eventually they loaded my sorry behind onto a plane and sent me back to the U.S.

We landed at the regular San Francisco Airport, and without a word they turned us loose to go home on 30-days' leave. Talk about a terrible mistake! I suspect that very few of us were in any kind of shape to reconnect with the normal world and with our past. We needed time and help to get our brains back to being able to deal with all of that. But no such luck. You got off the Pan Am flight and you were just flat out on your own... I guess I wandered over to where my flight back to Grand Rapids, Michigan was to take off.

As the book *The Spitting Image* documents, all those stories people love to tell about poor GIs like me just back from the war having mean old anti-war hippies spit on us are just myths. The image showed up in something like 60 movies about the war, but there are no, none, zero actual documented cases in the real world. In fact, my personal experience was almost exactly the opposite: I got accosted by some flag-waving patriot who wanted to make a big deal about how wonderful I and the war were in the faces of a small group of counterculture folks (long hair, beads, peace buttons, etc.) who were sitting minding their own business about 20 feet away.

He was only warming to the subject when I cut him off and told him the war was a crock of shit, the government was telling the American people nothing but lies, and that the war protesters were the real heroes. With that, I turned my back on him, walked over and asked the long-haired folks if they would mind if I sat with them because that John Wayne over there was getting on my nerves, and yes, I was just off a plane from Vietnam and I was so glad to once again be with like-minded people who know the war is a terrible thing that needs to be stopped. We had a very pleasant chat.

Once I got home I remember my mom was in the hospital, and I remember a drive my grandmother (my dad's mom) and I took. And that is about it.

My mom had had a back pain problem and had been prescribed some medicine for it. She reacted to the medicine, and so they prescribed something to help deal with that. She reacted to that, so they prescribed something to deal with that. She reacted to that, and on and on and on until she was taking about 16 different things, was down to about 90 lbs. and was curled in a fetal position and had nearly been given up for dead, until a new doctor walked in (about the time I got back in town), took one look at her chart, reportedly freaked out at how stupid his peers were, and took her off of everything. She began to improve immediately, and 40+ years later is still going strong.

My Grandma Arnold took me over to Fremont to meet the woman who was organizing anti-war protests up in that neck of the woods. At the time I had no idea why Grandma A. of all people would do that; she was about as patriotic as they come, but in retrospect I think the fact that every one of her kids (my Uncles David and John) and shirttail relatives who had been to Vietnam had come back saying pretty much the same thing, that the war was a crock, that it was being lost, and that the government was lying through its teeth about it, had finally started to get to her. She always had been very cool, as in good, smart, thoughtful, etc. I remember her once very sweetly breaking it to me (when I was maybe 8) that this very special rock I'd found "and was going to keep for ever and ever" was in fact a turtle turd. She could do that kind of thing and make you feel good at the same time, kind of like TV's Mr. Rogers.

In any case we hadn't called ahead, and the person we'd driven over there to see wasn't home, so we headed back to Big Rapids. Grandma was driving. The road twisted and turned a lot, and in the meantime quite a thunderstorm had started. It was getting dark, and as we came around a bend we barely were able to miss hitting a big tree limb that had fallen across most of the road. You could see where lots of people had driven over on the shoulder around it. But not Grandma. She said, "It's getting dark. If that isn't moved, someone will hit it and get hurt." With that, she pulled over, we got out, and she (then in her 70's) and I in the pouring rain pulled and tugged that big limb off to the side of the road. That was classic Grandma A. Something needed to be done, and she did it, for no reason except that it needed to be done.

I have no memory of the rest of that leave.

Chapter Fourteen
29 Palms

Reporting to Marine Corps Base 29 Palms, California was the usual ordeal. I knew it was out in the High Mojave Desert in the middle of nowhere somewhere east of Palm Springs, but that was about it. I flew to the nearest airport, which was Palm Springs, where I learned that there was exactly one bus per day that went from Palm Springs to that godforsaken place. By the grace of God, and not due to any planning or knowledge on my part, I arrived in time for that, and so I climbed aboard the old beat-up former school bus which made up 29 Palms Stagecoach Lines and got to the base within the time limits the Marine Corps had allowed for that.

Reporting in gave me pause. I went to the Base offices where one reports in, saluted the Duty Officer as one is supposed to, and announced as one must, "Corporal John M. Arnold reporting for duty, sir!" at which point someone in the big office area behind him said, "Oh, that is Arnold!" and the whole room turned to look at me! "This is not good," I thought to myself... But they just affirmed that I was indeed assigned to the 9th Comm Battalion, pointed out where they had their offices, and let me go. I wandered over there and reported in without incident.

By then I think the Marine Corps didn't know what the heck to do with me. I was a known problem (although the details of how and why I was a problem had been lost with my Naval Intelligence file), who nevertheless had gotten great Conduct and Proficiency scores and a promotion from both the unit where I reportedly had done much/most of my troublesome handiwork,[*] and from my unit in Vietnam. Was I a terror or a wonder? Who knew?

It turned out that the 9th Comm Battalion had a little problem of its own: They had a major inspection coming up, and apparently had not done very well the last time they'd had one, so really needed to do well this time. Unfortunately, one of their key players, the NCO who handled the Battalion's members' service record books and all discharge matters, was getting discharged himself, which would leave a big hole in a critical area for their passing that inspection. Since I couldn't work as a radio operator anyway, they appointed me his successor. He'd gone to school to learn how to do all the stuff related to keeping up service record books and doing discharges. We worked together for three days, and then he was gone, and that was all the training I got...

Fortunately, everything the job entailed was covered in great detail by this one big book called the "I.R.A.M.", which I know stood for something, but I don't recall what. In any case, the I.R.A.M. and I became bosom buddies. We very nearly ate and slept together as I put in 16 hour days checking every entry on every page in every service record book in my care (about 400 if I remember correctly) against what the book said should be there. The method to my madness was that if I could ace that inspection it would buy me protection should the outside world ever try to get at me. By happy coincidence the work was fun - kind of

---

[*]   In the meantime the Commandant of the Marine Corps, in testimony before Congress, had described my little group in North Carolina as having been "one of the most dangerous adversaries the Marine Corps had ever faced..."

like solving mysteries - and I turned out to be very good at it.

The guy I had replaced, who they thought was good, only had the books about 85% right, and there were some issues he had obviously never paid any attention to. I paid attention to EVERYTHING, and as a result of needing to get the CO to initial some of the changes and entries, he quickly caught on that I was catching a lot of stuff. One of the more interesting things was checking people's service history against the awards addenda that Headquarters Marine Corps would send out every month or so updating the I.R.A.M. on awards that had been approved after the fact.

For example, the Vietnamese Cross of Gallantry I have was awarded to all personnel who had been part of particular units at particular places within particular dates. I would track that stuff down, often finding that people qualified for as many as two or three more medals than they were aware of. It was the same with promotions, some of which were based on Conduct and Proficiency scores plus time in current rank. My predecessor had missed a lot of those, so not only was I pleasing and impressing the CO, but at the same time I was making some friends in the unit by getting them medals and promotions.

The inspectors came, and while they reportedly normally just spend a half hour to 45 minutes going over the books, they spent half a day on mine, searching nearly in vain for an error. Their oral assessment was that mine "were the best books on the West Coast," and in their written report the Battalion Commander got a commendation for the excellence of them. They (the books) got the highest score of all the things they checked in the Battalion. As a result I became the Battalion Commander's fair-haired boy, which meant that I could somewhat safely get back to working on the real business of the business, which was stopping the war.

The Marine Corps, bless its little heart, is pretty rigid. It has problems dealing with things that are unusual and unexpected. For example, suppose someone were to go to town on liberty and purchase a little can of something like spray paint, and suppose they used that can of spray paint to paint something like a peace sign on the side of something like a garbage dumpster. A normal organization or institution would just paint over it, but not the Marine Corps. They would have a crew out there for half a day measuring and photographing it and searching through the dumpster for evidence, and over the next day or two they would march hundreds of troops over to it and lecture them on the evils of subversion and "Fifth Columnists" in a complete overreaction all out of proportion to the incident. And as a result, within 48 hours, painted peace signs would spring up like magic all over the base.

Or, for example, suppose someone were to buy and leave out in a fairly public place some periodical known to expound liberal ideas; say, the Los Angeles Free Press. Again, a normal organization would pick it up and toss it in the trash along with other litter - but not the United States Marine Corps. They would take pictures of the scene of the crime, carefully analyze the contents of the offending publication, and then issue stern warnings to thousands of troops about the evils of such material, causing nearly everyone on the base to commit themselves to finding, buying, and abandoning on base as many such publications as possible.

The masterpiece, however, was the flagpole incident of May 1, 1971. The first day of May is traditionally celebrated around the world, primarily by leftist/liberation movements, as "May Day", a day to celebrate revolution and liberation. But not in the U.S., where it had been ham-handedly renamed "Law Day" and was a day when we were supposed to solemnly reflect on the importance of law and order, having been inspired to such thoughts by the President's Law Day Address. Richard Nixon extolling the virtues of law and order... Where is my air travel motion discomfort bag?!?

At 29 Palms, Law Day was observed by having the entire frigging base assemble itself around the main flagpole at zero dark thirty in the morning so that as soon as they put up the flag at precisely 0800 hours the Base Commander could read the President's Address and thereby inspire us all.

So everybody had to be there all polished up and ready for inspection a few minutes before 8:00 am. Just like in San Diego, the Colonels told their officers to get everyone there by 7:30 am. The Majors didn't want to fail to achieve that, so they told the Captains to have everyone there by 7:00 am. The Lieutenants didn't want to have their careers blemished by having their troops be late, so they told their staff NCOs to get everyone there by 6:30am, and so it went down the chain of command until in the end almost the entire base's population was standing around like idiots at 4:30 in the morning waiting for a stupid 8:00 am ceremony. There was, shall we say, a degree of hostility toward this whole event in the air right from the very beginning.

But stand around we did, until a little before 8:00

am when they called us all to attention, and the very stiff color guard marched over to the flagpole to ready things for raising the flag precisely at 8:00 am. Their person in charge had this gold key on a white braid around his neck, and he stiffly leaned toward the flagpole and inserted the key in the lock on the little metal box that covered where the rope was laced back and forth on some holder things. Or more properly, he attempted to insert the key in said lock. It quickly became apparent that he was experiencing technical difficulties with this maneuver. The key would not go in the lock. People in the ranks started giggling.

The Commanding General's face turned red, and the color guard started losing its stiffness as they tried to figure out what the problem was and how to help. Laughing started. The General snarled an order to an aide who stiffly but quickly marched over to the flagpole and demanded to know what the problem was. Now people were really getting into it as the color guard members frantically dug their fingers into the side of the little box and tried to pry it open. Nothing worked, and imperceptibly Law Day had become May Day, and 10,000 people were now glad they came for the show. The appearance of a crowbar was greeted with boos, but it did its job, and the flag was finally put up, and the President's speech was read, but that didn't matter. The people united will never be defeated!

A subsequent investigation found that sometime between when the flag was lowered the evening before and when the color guard tried to open the little box thing in the morning, some person or persons whose identity was never discovered had applied some glue-like substance such as epoxy to the lock, rendering it inoperable. Dang Fifth Columnists again!

Every so often the Base Legal Officer, a big lanky Texan, would be jogging around the place - he being one of those strange people who seem to enjoy jogging - and he would see me and come jogging over and slow down long enough to ask something like, "Is this the Corporal Arnold I keep hearing about?" I would quickly assure him that that would be my evil twin, Micky, and he would nod knowingly and suggest that I have Micky keep his head down for a little while so that things could blow over without he, the Legal Officer, having to do anything. I would promise to pass on that advice, he would grin, thank me, and go jogging on his way. Those were the only conversations we ever had.*

The nicest thing that happened during my nine months at 29 Palms wasn't at 29 Palms, but rather up in San Francisco: The anti-war movement was trying to pull off huge demonstrations on the East and West Coasts on April 24, (1971), and as we got closer to that date it appeared that the demonstrations were indeed going to be huge, so I applied for a weekend pass. This was a bit tricky because you have to say where you are going … "Oh, up to the San Francisco Bay Area..." ...and why… "To visit some friends (about 250,000 of them, to be exact!)" ...But be darned if they didn't give it to me without any hassles at all.

I flew up to San Franciso carrying the jungle utilities and boots I'd worn back from Vietnam, my medals, my "Vietnam Veterans Against the War" button,

---

*   He later resigned his commission and, at great personal risk, did a tremendous job reporting (possibly for the New York Times?) on human rights abuses committed by the Right Wing death squads the U.S. supported in Honduras, Nicaragua, and El Salvador during the Reagan years.

and a beautiful full-size flag (white with large peace sign) I'd bought. The ads for the demonstration said they would be helping people find housing, so I figured I would just look them up and let them do that. I rode the bus from the airport into downtown San Francisco and asked one of the guards at the bus station how to get from it to the demonstration's headquarters address. He said, "Go out the front door, turn left, go to the second building, and you are there."

So I went there, and sure enough there was a desk with a big sign on it that said "Housing Assistance." Unfortunately no one was sitting there, so I sat down myself, and in just a few minutes a guy came in and said that he could provide a place to stay for one or two people. I said, "Excellent, I am your person!" And that took care of that!

My host turned out to be a Vietnam Vet. from the Army. That evening we scrounged around the place where he lived and came up with a good flagpole for my flag. The next morning, the day of the demonstration, we went to where veterans and GIs were supposed to gather and were delighted to find ourselves in the company of maybe 10,000 other people. The demonstration was actually a march/parade of about 30 blocks through the heart of the city on a street that was 6-8 lanes wide. It was anticipated that so many people would participate (the final crowd estimates were about 250,000 people) that they couldn't all gather at one place, so along the route they had different kinds of folks gathering at different parks, and then as the front of the march (GIs and veterans) went past, they were to fall in behind.

There were parks for union folks, and Third World

people, etc, and it was all supposed to kick off at maybe 10:00 am. We'd gotten there early, of course, and sat around chatting with people as we waited for it to start. My flag was rolled up. The starting time came and went, but the organizer people who were running around talking on walkie-talkies (this was before cell phones) kept saying that we should wait longer so more people could get there; that they were expecting more people. This was okay for a while, but they were really obnoxiously bossy about it, and some of us had planes to catch, and after 30 minutes or so people started to get visibly restless. We were, after all, GIs and veterans, and having a bunch of snot-nosed civilian know-it-alls bossing us around did not sit well.

At about 45 minutes past when the march was supposed to have started, I announced to the dozen or so people right around me, "That's it. We're going!" and with that I stood up, unfurled my flag, which beautifully flapped open in the breeze, and started walking in the direction the march was supposed to go. A huge cheer went up, and in a heartbeat 10,000 people were up and moving, despite all the walkie-talkie bureaucrats shouting "Wait! Wait!" Waiting was over. We'll just be going now, thank you.

The crowd parted so that my flag and I could lead, and we funneled through this fairly narrow alleyway that emptied out onto the big main street we were going to be marching down. As we came out of the alley, what did we see before us but the other 10,000 veterans and GIs that the idiots with the walkie-talkies had been wanting us to wait for, who had been kept waiting by their walkie-talkie idiots waiting for us! In any case, another huge cheer went up, and 20,000 GIs and veterans chanting "What do we want? PEACE! When do we want it? NOW!" at the top of their lungs started marching six lanes wide through the heart of San Francisco.

Other flags of various sorts appeared as we went along, but by unspoken agreement the beautiful white peace flag I carried was the flag leading the parade. Besides, having a Marine color guard is traditional!

I cannot even begin to tell you how much fun and what a spiritual uplift that march was for me. 20,000 veterans and GIs equals two full military Divisions. That is a lot of folks. And that was only the beginning. Eventually another 230,000 or so people joined us in what was reportedly the largest peace demonstration ever held on the West Coast. It was eclipsed on the national news by an even bigger demonstration in Washington, DC (the one culminating in hundreds of Vietnam veterans tossing their medals on the White House lawn), but we didn't care. As we went up and down the hills you could look back and as far as you could see there was nothing but thousands and tens of thousands of people marching and singing and chanting for peace. It was just awesome.

A lot of media, some police, and a few crazies were up ahead of us, and we didn't really have a clear view of what was ahead of them, so it was of some interest and slight concern when the walkie-talkie folks started looking very worried and began running up ahead and forming a hand-to-hand human wall on an angle between us and something that was going to be coming up on our right.

Come to find out that it was the park where people who actively supported a Viet Cong/North Vietnamese/ communist victory in Vietnam had gathered. It was full of NVA, Viet Cong and Red flags of various sorts, and lots of signs supporting a victory by that side. Obviously the organizers feared that there could/would be trouble between that group and those of us who had served in the war. For just the slightest instant there was this cosmic pause as each group realized what the other one was, and at that instant I spun around and faced my 20,000 compatriots and at the top of my lungs chanted, "Ho, Ho, Ho Chi Minh! NLF (National Liberation Front) is going to win!" and 20,000 voices took up the chant.

The other group's faces registered incredulity, then joy, and then their voices took up the chant as well, and the two groups merged in one huge demand that the war be ended and that the right side win.

I was probably photographed a thousand times that day, and as an active duty Marine in full (albeit jungle utilities) uniform carrying a peace flag in an anti-war demonstration, that was not without its risks, but I didn't care. Whatever came of it, it was worth it. And as it turned out, nothing bad ever came of it.

Back at 29 Palms I was counting down the days. I just needed to survive until September 30 when my three years would be up. For some reason I did not elect to do as many of my peers and try to find some school I could sign up for that started within 90 days of the end of my enlistment. If you did that, they would let you out early so you could start that school; and as the discharge clerk for my unit I had to process those requests and discharges. There was a whole black market in school catalogs. Today everything would be on the internet, but back then it was a stream of school brochures that went surreptitiously from hand to hand. It didn't really matter what the school was; what mattered was that it start as close to 90 days from the end of one's enlistment as possible. Blacksmithing. Hair cutting. Truck driving. Charm and dance. I saw them all.

One Vietnam vet in our unit (who had initially enlisted for four years and so still had well over a year to go before he was supposed to get out) went at the problem slightly more creatively: He developed a series of quirky mannerisms, the most unsettling of which was following officers with a long, serious gaze while muttering over and over, "...If they don't let me out, I'm going to kill one of those motherfuckers..." It was a trip. You'd be walking along having a perfectly normal conversation and some officer would walk by and this guy would tighten all up and start staring at them and muttering. Finally it worked. They found some loophole and let him go.

But I was generally doing okay, so I didn't feel compelled to such extreme measures. I got along well with our Battalion Commander (we were not as close as with the crew in Vietnam, but he did favor me to the point of giving me 4.9 performance and conduct scores when I was discharged), though once again the unit's Executive Officer was a problem. He was so gung-ho that one of the things we had to do every day was make sure he knew when it was about 8:00 am so he could go stand outside and be ready to salute in the direction of the base's main flag pole when they blew the siren that meant they were raising the flag for the day. Obviously he hated me, but nothing really came of that until right at the end.

The people I worked with on a day-to-day basis were pretty decent. My only run-in there was a silly thing: The Staff NCO directly supervising us was a Sergeant Major who was an old infantryman who had been in the Marine Corps since World War II. He was a trip - very decent, but very Marine Corps. Straight as an arrow with at least seven rows of ribbons and a flat-top haircut, he was a living recruiting poster. We normally got along well. Then one day a silly situation developed when I had to process some guy for a medical discharge because of a condition or injury he'd gotten while in the Marines. There were only three kinds of ID cards available: Active Duty, Reserve Duty, or Retired. We had to give him one of those so he would retain his PX and military medical care benefits, etc. but none of them seemed a good fit, and for some reason, for the first and only time ever, poor I.R.A.M. didn't help me out with information deciding the matter.

I don't know whether he was having a bad day or what, but the Sergeant Major was not pleased when I asked him what he thought about it. He said it had to be the Reserve card. That clearly wasn't right, but he nearly bit my head off when I tried to explain why I thought it probably really should be the Retired card. It really wasn't a big deal, we would give the guy whatever card we decided to give him, he would go up to the Base offices with it, and if it was the wrong one they would send him back for the right one. But I just hated doing something wrong when it would be easy enough to do it right, so I called the Base's processing center and asked them.

They not only bit my head off, but then they called the Sergeant Major to complain that they had better things to do than tell his staff how to do their jobs, and wasn't that what he was supposed to do? He then proceeded to rip me up one side and down the other, letting me know in no uncertain terms that Corporals do not question the judgment of Sergeant Majors. So I issued the guy a Reserve card, we sent him up to Base, and they sent him back with a note essentially saying that even an idiot should know that he was supposed to have a Retired card.

I quietly typed that out and we gave it to him, and not another word was ever spoken about the incident, but the Sergeant Major never questioned my judgment again. This was especially true after I covered for him one day when he screwed up: The pay phone system in the town of Twentynine Palms was unusual in that you had to dial the number, the party you were calling had to answer, and then you had to put in your coins before the party you were calling could hear anything you said. The result was that fairly often we would get calls - usually from families of people in our unit who were in the area and wanted to talk with or see their loved one - where people would be fumbling with coins or whatever and there would be a long pause between when you picked up the phone and said, "Hello?", and when you could actually hear the caller say anything.

We who normally answered the phones knew that, but the Sergeant Major did not. One day he happened to be walking through and snatched up a ringing phone and barked, "Hello!", and when nothing was said in reply, he uttered a colorful phrase or two and slammed down the phone. A few minutes later, the Commanding General's office was on the line wanting to know who it was we had answering the phones for us? Apparently some Marine's mom had recently tried to call us, and before she could get the coins in the phone there had been some unpleasantness, and she wanted us to know that she was NOT what she had apparently been called. The Sergeant Major was standing right there when I took that call and turned beet red. I don't recall what I said, but I was able to smooth things over and save his hide.

As with the stupid ID card, nothing more was ever said about the incident, but he never grabbed a ringing phone again, and we got along well. My fondest memory of him was one day he wandered into the office area where a half-dozen of us peons were sitting at our desks working, and he was humming the song "I Feel Pretty" from the musical "West Side Story", which I assume he'd just heard on the radio or something. Anyway, here is this grizzled old Marine Corps Sergeant Major humming "I Feel Pretty" and all of us turned and looked at him. There was a second's pause, and then he realized what the very amused looks on our faces were all about, and he turned beet red and fled the room without a word.

Barracks life had long since lost any attraction for me, so a couple other guys and I pooled some money and rented a house out in the desert about a mile from the base gate. What I most enjoyed was walking to and from it, across the desert, generally late in the evening or early in the morning. It was breathtakingly beautiful, the plentiful scorpions notwithstanding. Our house had a little knee-high white picket fence around its front yard, and as we opened the gate and entered we would have a little ceremony the point of which was to leave the Marine Corps on the outside. Then we generally had a second ceremony, which was to turn over and shake everything (yard furniture, etc.) to find all the scorpions we had accumulated during the day (as many as half a dozen) and toss them out of the yard. It was pretty nice, but all of my housemates were pretty messed up with booze or relationships and eventually all of them got busted or went AWOL.

The other interesting incident with respect to the house was trying to get insurance on a car I bought for

$60 to make getting groceries, etc. easier. I went into an insurance company office in town and announced, "I'd like to get some insurance on my car." The guy looked up and said, "No you wouldn't." "I wouldn't?", I asked. "Let me put it this way," he said, and asked me four or five questions, about my age, marital status, etc. Then he punched some keys on his calculator and said the minimum coverage required by the State would run me $600 for six months. By gosh, I had to agree with him, I didn't want insurance after all! So I gave the car to a guy going off on leave, and asked him to just lose it someplace...

On base as an NCO I occasionally had to pull Duty NCO duty, which meant keeping the barracks residents under control for the weekend. Generally this just meant dealing with the sorts of things drunks normally do, the most common of those being half-waking up, having to pee, and wandering in a stupor almost anywhere to do that, including over to the next bunk, much to the dismay of the person who happened to be sleeping there.

Delightful duty, but only once did it get ugly: We had some extra barracks space and Reservists out for their two weeks of training would stay there, sharing bathrooms with our permanent residents. For some reason bad blood had developed between some of our people and these sojourners, and one night when I was the Duty NCO that played itself out in the form of four of our people, quite drunk, badly beating one of the visitors there in the bathroom. I called for an ambulance, called the MPs, and went looking for the thugs. By the time the MPs arrived, they were spread eagle in the sand outside in their underwear with various lumps and bruises all over them, possibly from the nightstick I was carrying.

Not long after that, I was at work one day when I heard something of a whoop from the Commanding Officer's office, and an incredulous and angry-sounding Executive Officer demanding "There must be some mistake!" The CO came out of his office beaming and handed me an announcement that I was to be awarded a Navy Achievement Medal with Combat "V", compliments of the 5th Marines. That is one of the medals a General pins on you at a big ceremony. What a trip! Although you've got to wonder what he (the general) is thinking as he reads that the award is being given because somebody "kept good records, organized files, and issued timely reports"...? I didn't care. It was a lovely surprise from my buddies of the 5th.

Summer turned to fall, the end was at hand, and then disaster struck: It seemed that the Inspector General of the Marine Corps was due to make his annual inspection of beautiful 29 Palms about two weeks after I was due to be discharged, and one of the things the base and my unit set to working on in getting ready for that inspection was to make sure that all troops could march reasonably well, and that all NCOs and officers could lead marching drill.

Apparently the Inspector General's team would be randomly selecting officers and NCOs and having them lead various units in marching drills. So fine, everyone who is going to be here for the stupid inspection needs to know how to do that stuff, but I won't be here so it's not a problem, right? Wrong. The Marine Corps apparently has difficulty dealing with concepts as abstract as that, so I ended up spending a couple of hours every day for a couple of weeks drilling and leading drill with all of our unit's other NCOs.

The only problem is that I can't drill or lead drill to save my soul. I try. God knows I try. But it just isn't in me. And they got uglier and uglier about it the closer we get to the stupid inspection date, to the point of threatening to bust any of us who couldn't get it right back to Lance Corporal. All of us who were at risk had gotten our second or third stripe in Vietnam where drill was not a big issue, so this struck us as a big flaming crock of you know what.

I don't know what other folks did, but I went to see my unit's Commanding Officer and pointed out to him that while I would NOT be here for the inspection, the office records WOULD be, and that it seemed to me that my time would be better employed in getting those records in shape instead of marching around in circles out on the parade grounds. Thankfully he agreed, and my Corporal stripes were saved.

Your last three days in the Marine Corps are supposed to be your own to use in getting ready to get out; doing stuff such as having to go see some officer about maybe reenlisting (Short interview in my case: Him: "You don't want to reenlist, do you?" Me: "No sir!" Him: "Dismissed!"), but the office I worked in was short-staffed, so I hung around there helping out instead of essentially just taking it easy which I had a perfect right to do. These were my buddies, and buddies help each other. Everything was fine until the Executive Officer who hated my guts walked in.

Now, out on the street an enlisted person would always jump to their feet and stand at attention and all of that sort of thing in talking with an officer, but when officers and enlisted people share a relatively small office space you normally don't do all of that in the interests of anybody getting anything done. So when he wandered up behind me early in the afternoon of my last full day and observed, "So you're getting out tomorrow, Corporal Arnold?" I just happily answered "Yes sir!" without standing up or even much looking up - at which point he jumped all over my case about not standing at attention when addressing an officer and just because I am getting out soon doesn't give me the right to disrespect an officer and blah blah blah in my face ending with an observation by him that in his opinion my mustache is too long and that I am to report to him at the flag-raising ceremony at 0800 hours the next morning with it shaved off. And, after making me admit that his orders to me were "clear", he went stomping off.

Everybody in the place was just scandalized. They all knew I'd put in my three years, including a year in Vietnam, and didn't even have to be in the silly office helping out so the unit would do better than it otherwise might in the inspection that wouldn't even take place until after I was long gone. What a jerk! I expressed my regrets to my coworkers that my ability to help them further was being summarily cut short and wandered into the CO's office with my discharge paperwork (which required his signature). As we chatted, I went on about what a blot it would be on the record if, after all the good work we'd been able to do together, he were somehow prevented from getting to the office in the morning to sign my paperwork then. A sickness. A car accident. An earthquake. Plague? Who knew what could happen? Why take the risk? Why not just sign the paperwork now? Laughing, he did. Laughing, I went off to pack.

My buddies from work insisted on taking me out for a farewell beer (which I don't drink) at the enlisted men's club (a place I avoided like the plague), which they liked but I hated. Why? Bad music played way too loud, vomit and fights. No, no, no, they protested; I must have just gone there on a bad night. It really is better than that. So we went, and when we opened the door to go in we were met with a blare of bad music playing way too loud. We sat down, and before anyone could even come over to take our order, someone barfed all over the table next to us. We moved to a different table, ordered, and a classic barroom brawl broke out at the table next to us. I thanked my hosts (who were laughing in embarrassment) for the lovely evening, and took my leave of them.

Back at the barracks I gave all my uniforms (except my jungle utilities and boots) to people who were going to need extra stuff for the inspection* and packed up what little I was taking with me.

At 0700 hours on September 30, 1971 I rode through the gates aboard the infamous 29 Palms Stagecoach Line school bus and bade the Marine Corps a fond farewell, commemorating that historic parting of the ways by tossing my razor out the window the minute we passed through the gate.**

* This was very much against regulations, since I was technically only transferring from active duty to the reserves and supposedly could be called back to active duty and would need those uniforms then. I assured people that where they would have to send me before I would ever come back on active duty again they have different uniforms for people to wear - either bright orange, or with black and white stripes - and so I was quite confident of not needing these particular uniforms anymore.

** Technically our evil Executive Officer could have sent a posse after me since he did, in fact, order me to report to him at 0800 hours that morning, which I did not do, and also to shave off my mustache, which I also did not do, and, if they wanted to get all picky about it, for leaving the base an hour before my discharge technically was effective,

And with that, I was a free man once again. I had served exactly three years to the day. I had gone in at age 17 and had gotten out at age 20. During those three years I had been promoted from Private to Private First Class to Lance Corporal to Corporal, and had been awarded: a Navy Achievement Medal, a Combat Action Medal, a Good Conduct Medal, a Vietnam Service Medal, a Vietnam Campaign Medal, a Vietnamese Cross of Gallantry, and a National Defense Service Medal. Although they had jerked my security clearance, my "infractions/disciplinary actions" service record book page was as clean on the day I got out as it was on the day I went in. And of course I got an Honorable Discharge. My head was a mess, and I felt 50 years old, but free at last, free at last, thank God Almighty I was free at last!

---

but I had a hunch that he wouldn't do that without the CO's okay, and that the CO who had just given me 4.9 conduct and proficiency marks probably wasn't going to give that permission. More likely he'd tell the XO to go salute the flag or something...

Chapter Fifteen
Back to Civilian Life

My sister was then married to a television actor, and besides their house in Van Nuys, California, they owned (or occasionally borrowed?) a house right on the ocean at Malibu. They wanted me to visit before I headed east, so we went up to Malibu.

The house was up on a cliff maybe 200 feet above beach level, with a little trail leading down to the beach, which was actually a series of small, more or less private beaches cut off from one another at high tide by big rock outcroppings. At low tide you could walk around them, and people often did, just strolling up and down the beach, as people will. The only difference here was that a significant percentage of those people did their strolling in the nude, a fact that was brought to my attention a day or two into my visit when I was sitting on the beach alone and two quite attractive young women, probably 16-19 years old, strolled by in such a state. They waved and said hi. I waved back, and suddenly realized that I had been so completely focused on the war that I had not given womankind a serious thought in three years. Clearly my mind was seriously messed up!

But the war was still going, and there was work that needed to be done, so at the earliest opportunity I set out for New York City where most of the big national anti-war organizations were headquartered. My dream was to work at the Vietnam Veterans Against the War national office, because as more and more Vietnam veterans were speaking out against the war it was clearly turning the county toward ending it. I knew that I wanted to be very active in VVAW, but that if I ended up having to work for one of the other groups to make money that would be okay too, so long as I could spend evenings and weekends doing VVAW things.

I flew in and somehow managed to get to Greenwich Village, where a sign on the front of the Greenwich Hotel proclaiming "Rooms - $1.00 per night" seemed to be just what the doctor ordered. I could stay there while I found a job and more permanent lodgings. So I went in and announced that I wanted a room. As with my car insurance misadventure in California, the desk clerk didn't bat an eye before insisting with equal certainty that I did NOT want a room. He went on to explain that the place was a dump, the rooms were ugly little cells, the plumbing at the end of the hall generally didn't work, and the residents were all bums.

I said it sounded lovely, and that I really did want a room. He allowed that, "it was my funeral", and took my $1.00. It was a colorful place, full of colorful people, and the location was great; it was on Bleeker Street (immortalized by Simon and Garfunkel in their song by the same name where "thirty dollars pays my rent") sandwiched, more or less, between the Avenue of the Americas and Washington Square.

The rooms were indeed spartan. They were about 7 feet long and probably only 5 feet wide. Whatever paint or wallpaper there might ever have been had long since largely fallen away. The floor was bare. There was a cot-like bed with a thin mattress and an even thinner blanket. There was a window, but it was broken (as in, half of it had no glass in it), which did tend to accentuate the cold at night. That was it - but what of it? I'd been in worse in Vietnam.

The next day I started making the rounds of the various peace groups, starting with VVAW, and was disappointed to find them all quite staffed to capacity with no plans for new hiring in the near future. I began pondering the possibility of needing to get a regular job and just doing peace work on the side. Bummer. In the meantime, the Vietnam Peace Parade Committee seemed nearly as disorganized as the original underground newspaper crew in North Carolina, so I started hanging out there, doing a little of this and a little of that, making myself useful.

My search for more permanent living arrangements was quickly dashed against the realities of New York rent rates. $1,000 a month to share an apartment in a bad neighborhood was not uncommon. In today's dollars that isn't too bad, but in 1971 that was a fortune, so although I kept looking, my hopes of finding anything wilted.

Back at the Greenwich Hotel, I and the other residents began sharing food (often cooked over little burners in the hall), whatever bottle was being passed around, what little toilet paper, soap, etc. that could be found, as well as apparently fleas.

Just a couple of days into my stay there I was sleeping one night when there was this very loud "BOOM!" It startled me awake, but it was the second "BOOM!" that sat me upright staring into the barrels of two NYPD police revolvers! The nearest cop demanded, "Where's the suitcase!?!" When that didn't register in my head as fast as he thought it should, he demanded again, "Where's the suitcase?!?"

By then I had sufficiently gathered my wits about me to suggest helpfully that my sea bag was under my bed. At which point the second cop suggested to the first one, "I don't think he's the guy, Harry. The guy that took the suitcase is old. This guy ain't old." They somewhat lowered their guns, and the first one asked, "You didn't steal a suitcase…?" "NO!" I affirmed. "Oh, okay. Sorry about the door…" they said, and left, leaving my door splintered on the floor… So I had to get up, get all my stuff packed, go down, get another room, and come back up. Definitely not the Ritz!

Over at VVAW I was on their speakers bureau, which sometimes worked out well, and sometimes not. One of the good times was when something happened in the national news that focused particular attention on draft resisters; probably some Nixon Administration official had suggested they were all cowards or something stupid like that. We got to comparing notes and it turned out that quite a few of us who were working in and around VVAW had enlisted at age 17, and so had never registered for the draft then, and had very intentionally not done so when we were discharged, even though the law required it, so we were all technically draft resisters!

We called a news conference which we all attended in full uniform with all our medals, and announced that in solidarity with our brothers who risked prison to stop the war, we too were intentionally in violation of the draft law and expected the government to do its duty and lock us up. Apparently they decided to pass on that opportunity.

The bad one was at, of all places, The New School, which is a very hip, up and coming University there in New York. We were asked to send five or six Vietnam vets over there to talk to a big rally about the war. So we went, and it was going okay until one of our group started talking about his personal hell: He had been out on patrol in hostile territory, came upon some hooches (huts), and heard a noise from inside one of them. Per standard operating (and survival!) procedures he'd hollered for whoever was in there to come out with their hands up. When no one did, he tossed a hand grenade in. It turned out that the hooch contained two small children, who his grenade blew to pieces.

He was in the middle of telling us about that when this very Bronxish woman's voice from the audience interrupted and said, "Excuse me, but can you tell me what time it is?" We were all so into this guy's story and the anguish he was living that we just all stared at her, which apparently made her angry, prompting her to admonish us that it was important that she know what time it is because "she has a class to go to!" We all just looked at one another and got up and left.

A few days later some group announced that it was giving some Nixon Administration official - one of the big outspoken war supporters - a "Humanitarian of the Year" award at a big gala event at Rockefeller Center in a couple weeks. Immediately groups started organizing a demonstration to protest it. All the big groups signed on, including the Peace Parade Committee. Since the Committee had not produced posters of its own to promote the demonstration, I thought it was great when some people from another group showed up and gave us a half-dozen big bundles of posters, free! The posters announced the demonstration in big letters, and then down at the very bottom in print almost too small to read they had that other group's name. The Peace Parade staff warmly thanked the delivery people, but dumped the posters in a trash can as soon as they were gone!

I freaked out and asked what the hell they were doing that for? "They (the group that had made and brought the posters) are Trots (Trotskyite socialists instead of whatever the hell kind of socialists the Peace Parade Committee people were)." I was so mad that I couldn't see straight. To hell with petty little ideological bullshit hairsplitting; there is a frigging war going on out there that is killing people! I got on the phone and called VVAW, and guarded the posters until a group from there came over and we carried them off to be posted on every telephone pole we could get to. That episode brought an end to my Peace Parade office volunteering.

The day (or more properly, evening) of the demonstration came, and so I put on my jungle utilities, ribbons, VVAW button, various other anti-war buttons, and took a long stroll up 5th Avenue to Rockefeller Center. New York demonstrations are weird: The police come and set up barricades around the space in which you are to demonstrate, and within that space you can do pretty much anything you want to, but the minute you step outside it, they can toast you. But they had given us a big space, including most of the sidewalk, the parking lane and probably halfway across 5th Avenue a whole block long right across the street from the place where the gala event was to be held. So we chanted and sang and marched back and forth to our hearts' content.

The demonstrators were a diverse group, including, somewhat to my surprise, people wearing football helmets, some body padding, face paint, etc., some of whom were also carrying large, sturdy walking sticks, which in Robin Hood's days one might have called staves. It seemed a little extreme, but hey, after living at the Greenwich Hotel for a few weeks almost anything could pass for normal with me!

During the evening I'd gravitated to the north end of things, and had gotten to chatting with some people I'd met there: another Vietnam vet who also lived in the Village, and some other people. We were just chanting and chatting and generally having a good time when much to our surprise the police started taking down the barricades. We looked around, and also much to our surprise we realized that most of our fellow demonstrators had left without our noticing it, and that the rest of them were in the process of leaving. So we said our goodnights, and the two of us from the Village started the long walk back south again.

We had only gone a short distance before we realized that not all was well with the world. Windows in buildings were broken. Trash cans and newspaper boxes were tipped over and out in the street. About the time the implications of all of that began to dawn on us, a running pitched battle came toward us from the south, winding itself through 5th Avenue traffic. In front were our friends in helmets, who were pausing occasionally to toss bricks or tear gas grenades through store windows or back at what was chasing them, which was a troop of New York's finest on horseback.

We were stunned. But as the melee approached we saw something that snapped us out of it real quick: Across from us a theater was letting out, and this very distinguished elderly gentleman and a woman, presumably his wife, had just stepped out onto the sidewalk. He was in a tux, she in furs and pearls. No matter. A cop rode up and let the old guy have it across the head with his nightstick. Smack! The man collapsed, his wife screamed, and we took off running - if they were smacking down old guys in tuxes, what were they going to do to the likes of us?!*

Rather than trying to explain to the police that we were peaceful demonstrators, we decided instead to scale the plywood wall around a construction site, drop down into the darkness on the other side, make our way quietly through the site to the next street over, and from there move over one more street, before furtively making our way south again.

By then my prospects for getting a peace-related job or a permanent place to live had dimmed to near oblivion, I was sick (just a bad cold, but I couldn't seem to shake it), my money was running out, and I was getting pretty tired of having fleas, so I decided that I would head back to Michigan and figure out my next step from there.

Back in Michigan, luck appeared in the form of a cooperative sporting goods wholesale distributorship my folks' and other little mom & pop sporting goods stores had started in Saginaw to supply stuff to them cheaper than the regular wholesale places would. It had a director person, but also needed a warehouse and paperwork person who would spend most days working alone while the other guy was out calling on stores, etc. Perfect! I didn't know anyone in Saginaw, and I found an apartment that was actually right above the first floor wholesale place, and just half a block from a fairly decent grocery store.

I could live, work, and be alone almost completely, and at that point in my life that is what I needed to do

*   I believe that news reports the next day identified the old guy as a member of the Board of Directors of Chase Manhattan Bank!

and be. I had no TV, no radio, no telephone. I knew no one, I socialized with no one, I lived alone. That was all I wanted, to be alone and not be around other people. Now we know to call this "Post Traumatic Stress Disorder", but back then all I knew was that being around other people creeped me out, and that more than anything else I wanted to be alone.

I came out of my shell only to campaign for George McGovern in the next fall's (1972) Presidential election in which Richard "bomb the Vietnamese back to the Stone Age" Nixon carried 49 of the 50 states. With that, I was through. That was the final straw. I quit my job, went back to Grand Rapids to get my stuff together and get a passport, and then I was leaving the U.S. for good. Period. It didn't matter where I went. I just wanted out of any country that could re-elect Richard Nixon and reaffirm his stinking war.

I helped out some at my folks' store while I was waiting for my passport to come, and one day a buddy of my brother came in. He was an Army Vietnam vet, and had also had some "readjustment" difficulties. We talked, and he suggested that before taking off for overseas I should take a drive out to Allendale where the State of Michigan had begun a really unique collection of little colleges all sharing the same campus. He said he thought William James College out there would be perfect for me.

I was seriously doubtful that anything in the U.S. could be even acceptable let alone perfect at that point, but he insisted that I give it a try, so I dutifully drove out there, where I was informed by a sign that William James College was housed in Lake Superior Hall, which some other signs got me to. I walked in the front door into a big space with some stairs going up to the second floor, a big painting of someone who I assumed was William James, and a couple of double doors leading off to the right and left, but no signs telling you where anything was.

I was about to turn and leave when one of the double doors pushed open and a dog (a Bearded Collie) came walking over to me. Very much in the spirit of Alice in Wonderland, I swear the dog (whose name I later learned was Mona March) used telepathy to ask me what I was looking for (I'm not making this up! And I wasn't doing drugs at the time...). I said I was looking for the Admissions Office. She seemed to say, "Okay follow me," and pushed back through the doors, and took me directly to the Admissions Office. I was enchanted. Maybe this would be an interesting place to be!

So I signed up for the winter term, paid for by Uncle Sam and the G.I. Bill. The College did indeed turn out to be a magical place, and the courses I was able to take my first term were balm for a very weary soul. But the war was still going on, and there was still work on it to be done, including mass demonstrations at Nixon's Inauguration, so I dutifully rode a chartered bus out to that, one of five buses from our campus alone, and as we headed east, more convoys joined us, and more, and more, until the whole freeway seemed filled with buses of demonstrators going to Washington to protest the re-election of this terrible man who was responsible for so many deaths.

The one thing we hadn't planned on was that it would be bitterly cold. It hadn't been that cold in Michigan, but it was freezing in Washington, to the point that staying alive became something one had to work at. The big parade came by, and large groups of Vietnam veterans silently stood and turned our backs as Nixon's limo passed. But Nixon was grinning from ear to ear and waving his hands in the air with his fingers making little "V's", and it got to one person sitting just a couple people over and in front of me. He snarled something about stinkingsonofabitch! and lunged toward the car, making it past two of the three rows of police before being brought down screaming and cursing. That was a little exciting.

I wanted to go to the White House to toss my medals over the fence as other Vietnam vets had in earlier demonstrations, but this time you couldn't get within three blocks of it, and my throwing arm isn't nearly that good! So in the end, not wanting to wear them back home again, I tossed them in one of the fires that people had started to try to keep warm. The people standing around the fire freaked out that I was doing that. Someone asked me if I wanted to say anything. I didn't. I couldn't. And that was that. I rode back to Michigan very depressed once again.

Just a few days later a very weird thing happened: I felt like I wanted to be around people, which was not something that I'd felt in years. So I wandered down to our dorm's TV pit, and settled in with about 30 other people to watch what turned out to be a terrible movie. They'd turned the lights out so you couldn't see anything but the TV, and most people just watched, but some of us kept making wisecracks about the movie. Two of us, to be more precise. And although we were enjoying each other's comments, other people kept shushing us, so eventually we moved next to one another so we could whisper our comments without bothering other people. And that is how I met Jeanne. And that is how I finally made it home from Vietnam.

She may remember it differently, but truly from that first meeting there never was anyone for me but her. We spent hours, hours, hours talking. Just talking, with me probably doing most of the talking, finally getting out all of the poison that had accumulated in my system for so many years. We married two years later, and the rest, as they say, is history.

I did continue to go to demonstrations, and even organized a few, including one where I handed Jerry Ford an anti-war pamphlet. My college dorm roommate (who had been exempted from the draft by virtue of being a conscientious objector) and I did some TV and radio talk shows together, with each of us supporting the other in our shared opposition to the war. And I certainly wrote a lot of letters to Congresspeople and to the media. Jeanne and I went to Kent State University for the memorial service of the 5th anniversary of the shooting of demonstrators there. But for the most part my involvement with the war was over. I'll likely never be completely over it; it has a way of creeping into my thoughts dozens of times a day even now forty years later. But the fighting did indeed end, I can once again function around other people, and I hope that history will vindicate the work that we of the peace movement did in trying to stop the Vietnam war.

Epilogue

John and Jeanne graduated from William James College in March, 1976, and moved to Springfield, IL. There they both worked for the ratification of the Equal Rights Amendment to the U.S. Constitution and on the legislative concerns of low-income people.

In 1982, John first heard of "food banks": nonprofit organizations that divert the food industry's usable discards from landfills to needy people. It was love at first sight. Over the next 28 years he directed three large regional food banks, overseeing the distribution of 321 million pounds of food aid and pioneering the use of more efficient and humane program models, including mobile food pantries and client choice.

In 2006, John was diagnosed with a malady common among U.S. troops exposed to Agent Orange in Vietnam: advanced, aggressive prostate cancer. *Peacemaking Under Fire* was completed as John was doing battle with Stage 4 of the disease.

69883414R00126

Made in the USA
Middletown, DE
10 April 2018